Government
of
God

Ron McKenzie
Kingwatch Books

Kingwatch Books
Christchurch
New Zealand
www.kingwatch.co.nz

Contents

Principles

This book sets out some important principles for the Government of God, but the practical outworking will vary according to local culture and living arrangements. People will have to work out the details by following the leading of the Holy Spirit and adapting the principles to their local situation.

Incomplete

Getting everything that needs to be in a book about the Government of God is almost impossible. I have concentrated on things that are new and different, rather than trying to cover everything that is relevant. For example, the arrangements I have described in this book must be undergirded by love and prayer, but I have not written much about these topics, because they are well-covered elsewhere. So if you think something important is missing, you might be right. I have probably left it out, because it is well understood, so just add what you already know to what you learn from this book.

Tough Read

Modern governments have such a big influence in our lives that most Christians will find it hard to imagine life without a powerful government. Most readers will find this book hard to swallow. Do not worry, because that is normal. Just put the book away in a safe place, and get it out when it becomes relevant. When darkness spreads, you will find its wisdom helpful. For the few who are ready to receive it, grab hold of the wisdom, and go for it with all your heart.

Preface

Follow the Authority

I was going to write a book about the Kingdom of God, but realised that it is so wonderful that a million books could not contain its glory. Authority is the heart of a kingdom, so to understand the working of the Kingdom of God, we must follow the authority. In this book, I focus on the aspects of life where authority is greatest.

In the modern world, most authority is political. Human political institutions exercise immense authority. There are very few limits on their authority. The coming of the Kingdom of God means a huge authority shift, so it will bring enormous changes to systems of politics and government.

Government is a process for exercising authority over society. Politics is a tool for deciding who should have authority to control people. The basic questions of political theory are:

- How should humans govern themselves?
- Who should have authority in society?
- How should authority be exercised?
- What gives governments authority to make people do things against their will?

Authority is at the heart of all these questions. The Kingdom of God provides a radically different answer to them.

A kingdom is a system for exercising authority and Jesus came proclaiming a new kingdom. The coming of the Kingdom of God requires a radical shift in authority, so it will have a dramatic impact on politics and government. In the last few centuries, human governments have accumulated immense authority. As God's kingdom comes to fullness, existing governments will shrink away and be replaced by a better government.

Trendy Words

Since I decided to follow Jesus forty years ago, I have been zealous for the kingdom of God. I wrote a book called the Glorious Kingdom in the 1980s, but no one was interested in the Kingdom back then, so it flopped. "Prophetic" was the popular buzzword at that time, with prophetic conferences and books on prophetic leadership.

A decade later, "apostolic" had become the popular adjective. Books were being written about apostolic government, apostolic leadership and apostolic reformation. That fad seems to have passed and "kingdom" has now become the adjective that everyone is using to describe what God is doing.

I am not sure that these trendy words mean much, because adjectives change, but the church remains the same. "Kingdom" is not an adjective that can be assigned to a church or a ministry. Kingdom is a noun. A kingdom is a people and territory with a king. In this book, I want to put some substance around the Kingdom of God and explain how it can become a reality on earth, not just a trendy adjective.

Clearing the Junk

God told Jeremiah that he had authority over kingdoms, "to uproot and pull down, to destroy and overthrow, to build and to plant" (Jer 1:10). This is always the way. God has to uproot and tear down the old, before he can plant and build the new. The same is true with the Government of God. The old ways of political power will have to be uprooted and torn down, before Jesus can plant his new government. Human governments will have to be overthrown and destroyed, before the Holy Spirit can build the Government of God.

Government of God

I want my readers to get a vision of what God wants to do, so I am not going to follow Jeremiah's example. Instead, I will follow Jesus' example and bring the good news first, leaving the bad news to the end. However, in history things happen the other way round. God will plant his kingdom among the trash, but he will have to clear it away before it reaches fulfilment.

Accordingly, this book has two parts. Part 1 is the substance of the book. It describes the nature and working of the new government that God wants to "plant" and "build". If you find yourself thinking as you read it, "This could never happen!", you might need to skip on to Part 2 to understand how all the obstacles will be removed.

Part 2 is about "uproot, pull down, destroy and overthrow". I describe the political junk that has contaminated God's world and prevented the Kingdom from emerging. I explain that modern politics and government have no place in God's plan.

I hate dwelling on this negative stuff, but these powers have been around for so long that we find it hard to imagine a world without them. Many Christians are so attached to political power that they will find it hard to let it go, so it must be exposed. Wrong thinking about government is so entrenched that it will have to be cleared away and replaced with the truth, before the Government of God can come.

We do not need to fight against political power. Instead, we should work quietly on the edge where they do not notice us and wait for God to deal with them when the time is right. The political stuff that clutters our culture will be swept away during a season of crisis. Our role is to be prepared with something better, so that God's kingdom can emerge in the rubble.

Living before the victory of the cross, Jeremiah focused mostly on "uproot, pull down, destroy and overthrow". Now after Jesus' victory and the outpouring of the Holy Spirit, the emphasis has shifted, so I have devoted fifteen chapters to planting and building the Government of God, with only three dealing with "uproot, pull down, destroy and overthrow".

Part 1

Plant and Build

1

New Government

One Government

Jesus began his ministry by proclaiming the arrival of the Kingdom of God.

> The time has come. The Kingdom of God is near. Change
> your thinking and believe the good news (Mark 1:15).

This was a radical message; far more radical than we realise. Establishing a new kingdom changes everything.

A kingdom is a territory ruled by a king. A territory cannot have two kings. If a new king gains authority over the kingdom, the old king is no longer a king. If a usurper invades a kingdom and defeats the reigning king, the old king must swear allegiance to the new one. If he refuses to submit to the new king, he would have to flee into exile to save his life. If he does not flee, he would be killed or kept in prison, so he cannot incite a rebellion.

The same is true in the modern world. When a new government gains authority, whether by war or election, the existing government loses authority and ceases to be a government. A government in exile is not a real government, because it has no authority in the nation.

A nation cannot have two governments.

When Jesus said that the kingdom of God was at hand, he was announcing the arrival of a new king. If the authority of this new king were accepted, existing authorities would have submit to him, or flee the territory. If his kingdom expanded throughout the earth, there would be no place left for them to exercise authority.

The kings, governors, priests and nobles who exercised authority in Israel understood what was happening. They realised that the coming of this new kingdom would bring a shift in authority in Israel. If the Kingdom of God gained authority, they would lose authority, power and privilege. This is why Jesus' authority was frequently challenged.

Herod recognised the threat, as soon as the wise men announced that a new king had been born. The threat to his authority was so serious that he massacred all the boys born in Bethlehem over two years.

> Herod was furious, and he gave orders to kill all the boys in Bethlehem and its vicinity who were two years old (Matt 2:16).

Jesus was just a baby, but he was dangerous to Herod, because he represented a challenge to his authority. Herod used ruthless power to eliminate him, but he failed. He took this brutal action, because he knew that his kingdom could not survive, if a new king established his kingdom.

Jesus' gospel was also a challenge to the authority of the spiritual powers at work in the world. They tried to get him to submit by tempting him in the wilderness, but Jesus resisted their tricks and was strengthened by the angels. Jesus cast out demons to demonstrate his authority over them.

> The people were all so amazed that they asked each other, "What is this? A new teaching—and with authority! He even gives orders to impure spirits and they obey him" (Mark 1:27).

The principalities and powers that controlled Herod and Pilate stirred them up to kill Jesus, because he threatened their authority.

Radical Change
One kingdom cannot exist within another. If there are two kings, one will dominate the other, who ceases to be a king. King Herod appeared to have a kingdom, but he was not a real king. He was

really just a governor appointed and controlled by Rome. They gave him the title "king", so the local people would accept him, but he had to obey the instructions of the Roman Emperor.

The Kingdom of God and the kingdom of man are totally opposed to each other, so they cannot operate in parallel. One must be dominant. The Government of God cannot exist under human government, because God would not be a real king. He is not interested in being the puppet of a more powerful ruler.

Likewise, human governments want to be dominant in everything, so they will not serve under God's authority. The Government of God must replace human governments.

The fullness of the Kingdom of God will be a massive challenge to the politicians and governments that dominate the modern world. They will be swept away and replaced by something new, different and better. When the Government of God comes, there will be no place left for human government. They will collapse and be replaced by the Government of God.

Jesus' message was unique and radical. He did not tell kings and politicians to operate in a different way. He rendered them redundant. His resurrection confirmed that he is Messiah, Lord and King. These are political terms. Where Jesus is Lord and King, human political powers and governments are obsolete.

The coming of a new kingdom shifts authority. The new king gains authority and the previous king loses his authority and has to flee with his supporters. Everything in the territory will change. The coming of the Kingdom of God requires a radical shift in authority, so it will have a huge impact on political power.

Authority Shift
Over the last couple of centuries, human governments have been given immense authority by the people of the world. Modern governments have accumulated immense authority, including:

- monopoly on law-making,
- monopoly on defence,
- monopoly on coercion,
- monopoly on justice.

For most of history, this authority has been controlled by human governments. They claim authority over every person and every activity that takes place in their domain. The coming of his Kingdom will shift all this authority back to God.

> The Lord is our judge,
> the Lord is our law-giver,
> the Lord is our king;
> it is he who will save us (Is 33:22).

In the Government of God, Jesus will be judge, law-giver and king. The coming of his Kingdom will shift authority on earth.

Many Christians have failed to understand the implications of Jesus' death, resurrection and ascension. They want to tinker with the current system of power by electing nicer politicians and changing laws. Jesus is not interested in tweaking the political system to make it function better. As his gospel advances, human political power will be replaced with a better government.

Government of God

Jesus is king in the Kingdom of God. We miss the full implications of this wonderful statement, because we do not understand the role of a king. Modern kings are wheeled out on special occasions, but they have no real authority in their kingdom. These rock star kings give a distorted view of kingship.

In Jesus' time, a king wielded the same absolute authority as is exercised by a modern government. To understand what Jesus meant by the word Kingdom, we should think about the authority of the modern state. There are no limits on what modern governments can do. They can legislate for every aspect of life and can levy taxes on any income or property. Modern governments have absolute authority. In Jesus' time, the same absolute authority was held by kings and emperors.

In a world without kings, the Greek word translated as kingdom would be better translated as "government". Everyone in the modern world understands the concept of government. We would get a better understanding of what Jesus meant by the Kingdom of God by thinking of it as the Government of God.

If Jesus had come in our time, he would have announced that the Government of God is at hand. Using this expression sharpens his message.

> The time has come. The *government of God* is at hand. Change your thinking and believe the good news (Mark 1:15).

> I must proclaim the good news of the *government of God* to the other towns, (Luke 4:43).

> He welcomed the crowds and spoke to them about the *government of God* (Luke 9:11).

> Jesus travelled about from one town and village to another, proclaiming the good news of the *government of God* (Luke 8:1).

In a world where most people are fed up with their government, an announcement of a new government is good news. The coming of a better government is extremely good news.

When we first hear the expression government of God, it seems odd. The thought of the Government of God expanding throughout the world sounds strange to our ears, but that was Jesus' message. He announced that the Government of God is near and promised that it will expand until it fills the whole earth.

The Government of God is not good news for everyone. Many people will not be that comfortable with the idea of God exercising the authority of a modern government. However, God exercises authority in a different way to human kings. He does not enforce his authority, but waits on people to freely submit to him because they love him and want to obey him. When the Kingdom of God has come, he will have authority over everyone, but it will be authority freely surrendered by people who love him.

The expression Government of God grates a little, so I will use it sparingly in this book. Most of the time, I will refer to the Kingdom of God, but I will mention the Government of God occasionally as a reminder that this is what it is.

Better Way

Political philosophers claim that government is necessary to bring peace and order in the world. Many Christians support this view. They agreed that life on earth would have been worse without government power. However, that claim is never proven, and history suggests that the opposite is true.

Human governments have failed totally in their efforts to provide peace and order for the world. They have done terrible evil throughout human history. Millions of people were killed and robbed by kings and their armies. Even more harm has been done by democratic governments. The most destructive wars in human history have occurred in the age of democracy.

We need a better way. Jesus began his ministry by announcing good news that a new government had come (Mark 1:14-15). The gospel of the Government of God promises to transform society without war and political power. Hearts will be changed first. As people freely surrender to Jesus and obey his word and the leading of this Spirit, society will be transformed from below.

God's system of government is the only solution that will work, but it has never been tried. This book describes how the Government of God could bring peace to our troubled world. It will replace the four main roles of modern governments.

- *Justice* was not important for kings. They did enough to prevent rebellion, but focus on rewarding their own people. Modern governments have made justice complicated and expensive. God's justice is described in chapters 6-11.
- *Social welfare* is a new role for governments. Kings did not care about the poverty. Modern governments have taken this role over from church and other social groups. Chapter 12 describes God's approach to welfare.
- *Defence* has always been the main role of kings and governments. Kings focused on protecting their own position. I describe God's approach to defence and protection in chapters 13-14.
- *Economic management* is a new role for governments. Kings did not see this as their responsibility, but modern governments are committed to establishing economic stability and growth. This topic is outside the scope of this book, but will be covered in my next book called God's Economy.

2
Different King

The character of the king determines the quality of a kingdom. A kingdom controlled by an angry and violent king will be characterised by violence and power struggles. A good king will bless the lives of his people.

A good king makes a good kingdom.
An evil king produces a bad kingdom.

A kingdom reflects the personality of the king. A new king with a different heart will transform a kingdom. The kingdom of a king who is loving and kind will be full of love, joy and peace.

Jesus preached the good news of a new king, and a new kingdom. A profoundly different king brings a radically different government. Jesus' Kingdom will transform every society.

Authority is the essence of a kingdom, so the coming of the Government of God will bring a massive shift in authority. God is a different type of king, so the exercise of authority in the Government of God is totally different to anything we have seen in the kingdoms of men. (The nature and working of authority is described more fully in my book called Kingdom Authority).

Types of Authority
Authority can take two main forms:
- Imposed Authority;
- Free Authority.

These two types of authority are distinguished by their source. Most authority that we experience in this world is imposed from above with force and power. I call this Imposed Authority. The other type of authority is created through voluntary submission by people under authority. Although it sounds like a contradiction, I call this Free Authority.

Free Authority

The main feature of Free Authority is that it is never enforced with power or coercion. The person making the decisions and issuing commands lets people choose whether to obey or not. People with Free Authority rely on the loyalty of the people under their authority to get their will done. Free authority is the best kind of authority because it provides the benefit of authority while leaving people free.

Free authority is created when one person agrees to submit to another. Free Authority is created by "voluntary submission". When a group of people freely submit to a person, they create authority that did not previously exist.

Free Authority is voluntary and temporary. It is voluntary, because the person with authority cannot demand it. The authority is temporary, because the people submitting can take it back at any time. If they stop submitting, the Free Authority disappears. Free Authority is controlled by the person who submits. They specify the scope and term of the authority they are surrendering.

Free Authority is fragile. If a person exercising Free Authority gets too oppressive, it quickly changes into Imposed Authority. People exercising Free Authority are accountable to the people who have submitted to them, so they must provide sufficient benefit to maintain their loyalty. For example, employers must pay wages, or their employees will resign. If the expected benefits are not forthcoming, voluntary submission can be withdrawn.

The Government of God is based on Free Authority, because God refuses to impose his authority by force. This radically different approach to authority makes his government unique and special, because it preserves human freedom. If people freely submit to God, because they love and trust him, they have given him authority over their lives. However, they are still free, because they can take back their authority at any time.

Love and submission meet perfectly in Free Authority, so it flows to good leaders. The disciples gladly submitted to Jesus, because they recognised his wisdom and knew he loved them.

The ultimate human freedom is submission to the Holy Spirit. When we submit to him, we give him authority over our lives. He loves Free Authority, so we gain all the wisdom of God, but continue to be free. Rebellion against the Spirit destroys freedom, because it gives the powers of evil authority in our lives. They twist it into Imposed Authority and rob our freedom. Voluntary submission to the Holy Spirit produces true freedom.

Imposed Authority

Imposed Authority exists when a person with authority has the power to enforce their will on others. That power might be the military power of a mighty empire. It may be the power of a gun, or simply bigger fists. Most human authority is Imposed Authority, maintained by coercion and enforced with physical power. The greater the physical power, the greater the authority that can be imposed.

Human kings have always used Imposed Authority. They could only maintain their position if they had a powerful army of loyal soldiers ready to enforce their authority. The army punished anyone who refused to obey the king's decrees. The king had to be physically tough to keep the respect of his soldiers. If he showed any sign of weakness, a strong soldier might start a rebellion and seize his throne by force.

Modern systems of government are based on Imposed Authority. Political leaders have access to extensive powers of coercion. They fund their programs with compulsory taxation. Parliaments have passed thousands of laws and applied millions of regulations that citizens must obey, even if they do not like them. When bureaucrats issue regulations, citizens must comply with them, even if they will be disadvantaged. People who refuse to obey have their property confiscated or are put in prison.

This gigantic accumulation of power results from expectations that governments can solve all the problems of the world. Big promises of big salvation need big control. The people of the world accept loss of freedom, because they believe the grandiose promises of politicians to solve all their problems.

Christians have gone along with this build-up of power, because they hope for the chance to use it, but it is really an expression of lack of faith in God. Imposed Authority always turns ugly, because it always needs more and more power.

Jesus could have called a legion of angels to enforce his authority (Matthew 26:53), but he chose to suffer on the cross to gain Free Authority. God will never force people to obey him against their will, so the Government of God cannot be established by Imposed Authority.

God wants authority submitted from below by people who have freely chosen to love and serve him. His Kingdom comes when the gospel has been successful and human hearts have changed by the presence of his Spirit.

Whereas God respects and protects human freedom, the devil is an expert at imposing his authority on people. He uses spiritual power to force those who belong to him to obey his will. He uses Imposed Authority to control everyone caught in his clutches.

No Delegated Authority

Christians have developed a doctrine of delegated authority to validate human political power. This doctrine claims that God has delegated authority to the political institutions that exercise power in modern society. Christians are expected to obey these authorities, because their authority is delegated by God. However, the claim that God has delegated authority to political powers is a distortion of the truth.

God never delegated authority to any human institution. He gave authority over the earth to Adam and Eve. Humans can pass their authority on to organisations and institutions by submitting to them, but God could not give human institutions and organisations authority, because he had already given all authority to the people on earth. No human institution has been delegated authority by God to control the rest.

To support the claim that God has delegated authority to their governments, Christians often say that he created governments in order to maintain order on earth until Jesus returns. They claim violence and chaos would take hold and life would be impossible without governments to hold it back. They never prove this claim and just ignore the death and violence that has been caused by political institutions.

God needs order on earth for the gospel to advance, but he has not delegated authority to political powers for this purpose. Law is a far more effective way to constrain the worst effects of sin.

> We know that the law is good if one uses it properly. We
> also know that the law is made not for the righteous but
> for lawbreakers and rebels (1 Tim 1:8-9).

God's law cannot eliminate all sin and evil, but if applied correctly, it can maintain order among sinful and rebellious people; something human governments have never been able to achieve.

Beautiful Kingdom
God has decided to establish his Kingdom on earth using Free Authority. This decision places huge limits on his ability to work in human history. Many of his followers do not understand this choice and expect him to impose his will on the world. Because he relies on Free Authority, he cannot just intervene when he chooses, but must wait for people with authority to invite him.

Jesus' death, resurrection and ascension opened the way for the Government of God. When he sat down at the right hand of his Father, Jesus sent the Holy Spirit to work with his followers to establish his government on earth. The Holy Spirit will bring in a beautiful Kingdom. He works in the hearts of all people to convict them of sin and to testify to Jesus. He draws people to Jesus and gives them a new heart. He guides them into all truth and teaches them how to live.

As the Holy Spirit teaches people to love and obey Jesus, all authority on earth will be brought into submission to him. The fruits of love, peace, patience, kindness and joy will dramatically change life on earth.

The Holy Spirit will establish the Government of God using Free Authority by inspiring people to love and obey Jesus. There is no need for coercion when he is free to work.

> "Not by might nor by power, but by my Spirit," says the
> Lord Almighty (Zech 4:6).

This beautiful kingdom will come as people choose to submit to Jesus and freely obey the prompting of the Holy Spirit. His authority will not be imposed by force, but will be won by love.

Jesus used power against demonic powers and evil spirits, but he refused to enforce his authority over people. His Kingdom is based on love and service, not on power. He refused to use force and coercion to get his will done.

Jesus called people to join his movement. Some left everything to follow him, but others thought the cost was too great. Those who chose to follow him were free to leave at any time, and many did. He did not threaten those who left, but sadly let them go. Even when he knew Judas was going to betray him, he did not try to impose his authority over him. He did not threaten him with perdition. Instead, he loved and served him to the end.

God's commitment to Free Authority means that the Government of God is fundamentally different from any other government ever seen on earth.

Changing the World

There are two ways to change the world.

- top down
- bottom up.

Modern movements to change the world try to influence politics and government. Authority comes from the top down, so everyone assumes that society must be changed from the top. Therefore, most modern attempts to change the world link with political power in one of its various forms.

- Start a new political party
- Lobby the political parties

- Elect a new president
- Get better people into parliament
- Pass more laws
- Stiffer penalties
- Spend money on social issues
- Develop a social program
- Overthrow the government
- Let the people seize power.

These solutions represent change from the top using Imposed Authority. They have been tried in different places at different times, but always fail, because society cannot be changed from the top down.

- Replacing one set of rulers with another changes nothing, because the same principalities and powers remain in control.
- Defeating an evil government by military force releases the spirits of control and violence, which undermines the Kingdom of God.
- Using democracy to topple political leaders strengthens human authority, which opposes the authority of God.

The Kingdom of God cannot be enforced from the top, because Imposed Authority allows the spiritual powers of evil to control an entire society by concentrating their attacks on a few powerful people. By controlling the political powers, they control everyone under the Imposed Authority.

The Government of God is based on Free Authority, so change comes when the people of the world freely choose to obey Jesus. His authority grows, as people hear the good news and freely choose to love and serve him.

Control

The big issue in discussions about political authority is who gets control. During the time of Jesus, the Roman Empire was in control. The early church was persecuted by the empire because it refused to recognise its authority.

With the conversion of Constantine, control shifted to Christians. For more than a thousand years, political leaders were Christian, or powerfully influenced by the church. At times, people who opposed the power of the church were persecuted.

In the last five hundred years, western society has become increasingly secularised. The influence of the church has declined, and fewer political leaders are Christian. Christians have lost control, so getting it back has become a big issue.

In a world of democracy, two ways of obtaining influence are commonly suggested.

- Getting Christians elected to political power.
- Persuading politicians to change policies that conflict with Christian standards.

Both options are wrong, because they attempt to restore Christian control of political power. The real problem is not lack of influence, but the nature of power itself.

Political power is always wrong, because it relies on Imposed Authority, which is contrary to God's way. Christians who seek to control it are aligning themselves with Imposed Authority, which has no place in God's plan. We must not attempt to use political power for Christian purposes. Instead, we should look for solutions that rely on Free Authority.

On the other hand, Christians should not try to destroy political power, because that would require the use of violence and Imposed Authority, which would make the situation worse. Only God can destroy political power.

3

Perfect Government

Jesus came to establish the Government of God. Because he is a radically different king, his kingdom will be very different from every other kingdom that has ever existed.

Although "government" is the essence of a kingdom, Jesus never said much about how his kingdom would be governed. The Sermon on the Mount announced a new set of blessings that are the outcome of the new government. However, he did not describe how government would function in his Kingdom.

The reason that Jesus did not introduce a new system of government is that God had already given a perfect system of government to Moses when he appeared on Mount Sinai. Jesus did not explain how his kingdom would be governed, because God had already given his perfect government.

Looking in the Wrong Place
Christians seeking wisdom about government naturally look in the gospels. However, they are usually disappointed, because the gospels record Jesus talking about the Kingdom of God, but they say very little about systems of government. The gospels contain plenty of teaching about what is just and unjust, but there is no guidance about a system of justice. They record Jesus' judgment on leaders collaborating with Rome, but are silent about what should replace them.

Jesus challenged the authority of human governments, but he never offered an alternative system of government. He did not need to, because he understood that God had already given his ideal system through Moses. God did not need to introduce a different system of government. Rather, he provided wisdom, insight and the gift of the Holy Spirit to help his people implement the system that God had already given.

The New Testament letters do not help those looking for a better system of government. Paul focuses on the advance of the gospel and the growth of the church. He had strong views about justice, but did not need to develop a new political and social theory in his letters, because he understood what God had given Israel when they moved into the Promised Land. He took this social and political system for granted and assumed it would be restored wherever the gospel was received. This is confirmed in his letter to the Romans (explained in chapter 9).

God had already given a complete description of his perfect government, so he did not need to repeat it in the New Testament. Instead of starting afresh, the New Testament writers looked for the restoration of the system of law and justice that had been given earlier, but rejected.

Those who cannot find a new system of government in the New Testament often go back to the Old Testament prophets, but this does not get them much further. The prophets made many declarations about injustice. They described the evils of the kings on Israel and Judah, and warned of judgments against the surrounding nations. However, the prophets never describe a better system of government.

When dealing with political and economic issues, the scriptures always look back to the system of justice and government that God gave to Moses. His ideal government is described in the scriptures, but we have not found it because we have been looking in the gospels and the prophets.

Missing Government

When they fail to find a "Christian" system of government in the scriptures, Christians assume God does not have one, so the best they can do is make existing forms of government work better. This is a mistake. God does have a perfect system of Government, but we will not find it looking in the wrong place.

God gave a perfect system of social organisation and government to Israel through Moses. In Egypt, the children of Israel had lived as slaves, so they did not need their own government. When they entered the Promised Land, they had to learn to live together in freedom. God gave them a perfect system of government and promised that it would bring great blessing. He has never given a better system.

We have been taught that the Law of Moses was a failure, so this is a difficult idea to grasp. However, the law failed as way of justification, but it did not fail as a system of government, because it was never really tried.

Human Government Preferred

Christians with an interest in politics and economics have a serious problem. God has given his people a perfect legal and economic system, but most do not know about it. God's system is described in the books of Moses, but most Christians do not like the Old Testament law, so they have opted for human systems of government instead. Two thousand years have gone by since Jesus said the Government of God is near, but the church has never bothered investigating God's system of government, so the world is still dominated by unreliable human governments.

For most of those two thousand years, Christian leaders supported human kings as the best form of government, even though the prophet Samuel had explained clearly that kingship was not part of God's plan (1 Samuel 8). More recently, Christians have advocated democracy without, realising that the rule of the people is the opposite of the Government of God.

God's system of justice and government was rejected by Israel, but it is still God's ideal. He has not changed his mind and thought of something better. We might not like it, but if we want to find God's perfect system of government and justice, we must go back to the books of Moses.

Government of God

Anyone who is interested in political theory and justice must study the Old Testament and gain an understanding of the perfect system of justice and self-government that God announced through Moses. Praying the prayers of David is the key to understanding God's system of government.

> Oh, how I love your law!
> I meditate on it all day long.
> Your commands are always with me
> and make me wiser than my enemies.
> I have more insight than all my teachers,
> for I meditate on your statutes.
> I have more understanding than the elders,
> for I obey your precepts (Psalm 119:97-100).

> Great peace have those who love your law,
> and nothing can make them stumble.
> I wait for your salvation, Lord,
> and I follow your commands.
> I obey your statutes,
> for I love them greatly (Psalm 119:165-167).

> I long for your salvation, Lord,
> and your law gives me delight (Psalm 119:174).

> The law of the Lord is perfect,
> refreshing the soul.
> The statutes of the Lord are trustworthy,
> making wise the simple.
> The precepts of the Lord are right,
> giving joy to the heart.
> The commands of the Lord are radiant,
> giving light to the eyes.
> The decrees of the Lord are firm,
> and all of them are righteous.
> They are more precious than gold…
> in keeping them there is great reward (Psalm 19:7-11).

Jesus announced a new king and a new kingdom. When describing how it would be governed, he linked back to the system of government and justice that God had given to Moses. When describing the nature of justice, he drew out commands from the Law of Moses and radicalised them. His new commandment was a rework of a command from Leviticus 19:18.

Jesus came to restore the perfect system of government that God had already provided. At the beginning of his ministry, he confirmed God's faith in the system of government that he had already given.

> Do not think that I have come to abolish the Law or the Prophets; I have not come to abolish them but to fulfil them. For truly I tell you, until heaven and earth disappear, not the smallest letter, not the least stroke of a pen, will by any means disappear from the Law until everything is accomplished (Matt 5:17-18).

Jesus was not contrasting law with grace. He was affirming the system of government that God had given through Moses and confirmed through the prophets.

Once we understand the perfect system of law and justice that God gave to Israel, we can understand how the gospel can empower it to make it relevant to the modern world.

Safe Society

A well-functioning society needs four basic things from a system of government.

- A process for settling disputes without resorting to violence.
- Protection from theft of property.
- Protection from assault and violence.
- Defence from attack by external military force.

No human system of government has ever provided all these things. God's perfect system of economic and social organisation offers them all.

God's perfect government has two main components:

- A way of justice;
- A way of defence.

The way of justice is God's laws for society applied by local judges. Every civilised society needs law to function well. God has met that need by providing a set of perfect laws. His law is "holy, righteous and good" (Rom 7:12). The foundation for perfect government is God's laws for society.

The second prong of God's system of justice is wise local judges. Law has to be applied. Good law needs wise judges to apply it. However, judges do not need to be appointed by political powers. In God's system, judges emerge within local communities as people take their problems to wise people. Local judges emerge as wise people develop a reputation for wise decisions. Good judges will be recognised by their neighbours.

Law and judges deal with three of the concerns listed above: disputes, theft and violence. Alongside his perfect system of justice, God gave a perfect system of defence, based on temporary military leaders. They deal with the fourth problem listed above.

When the children of Israel faced a threat, people from local communities would gather to defend themselves. Each group would appoint their leader. The leaders of hundreds and thousands would then appoint a military commander to lead them in battle (Moses was the first person in this role). When the threat had passed, the defenders would return to their homes and the temporary military leader would step down from their role.

God's system of government does not produce perfect people. Only the gospel and the Spirit can do that. However, it does allow imperfect people to live together in the relative harmony of a peaceful society.

Voluntary System

God is committed to Free Authority, so he will establish his kingdom on earth without using force and coercion. To achieve this goal, he gave the children of Israel a legal system that does not need political power. A key feature of his system is that no person or group of people is given authority to control society.

God's law provided a way for people to live together in society without needing Imposed Authority. Political power is not needed, because everything is voluntary.

- Authority to tax does not exist in God's Law, so there is no revenue for funding government activities.
- Executive authority is not covered in God's law. Presidents and prime ministers are missing. The kings and emperors of the surrounding nations had hierarchies of governors and officers. Nothing similar was authorised in the law.

- Moses was a temporary military leader. He was succeeded by Joshua, but no one succeeded Joshua, because their task was complete once the people were in the land.
- Government bureaucracy does not exist in the Law. No government agencies are authorised. There is no department of defence. The only permanent roles in Israel were the priests and the Levites. The priests managed the temple and the Levites had an education role. They were supported by voluntary donations. They had no authority to provide government services.
- The Law did not authorise a police force. There was no taxation to fund one. Enforcement of law was the responsibility of local communities.
- Government programs are not justified by the Law, because there is no taxation to fund them.

Light to the Nations

God gave his perfect system of government to Israel for their benefit, but he also expected it to be copied in the rest of the world. Moses explained,

> I have taught you decrees and laws as the Lord my God commanded me, so that you may follow them in the land you are entering to take possession of it. Observe them carefully, for this will show your wisdom and understanding to the nations, who will hear about all these decrees and say, "Surely this great nation is a wise and understanding people." What other nation is so great as to have their gods near them the way the Lord our God is near us whenever we pray to him? And what other nation is so great as to have such righteous decrees and laws as this body of laws I am setting before you today (Deut 4:5-8).

If Israel had implemented God's system, they would have become a light to the nations. The nations would have looked and seen that God's system of government brought blessing and peace to his people. They would have been amazed at the wisdom of God and realised that his system of government is better than what they had. Some nations would have been so impressed that they would have chosen to copy it.

Unfortunately, this never happened, because Israel rejected God's system of government and chose to have a king like the other nations. Instead of being a light to the nations, they adopted the darkness of the nations. This led to disaster, as they were harassed by stronger kings, and eventually forced out of the land by a powerful empire. They failed their calling and lost the blessing that God had promised.

Jesus launched a movement that would restore God's system of government, but the Jewish people rejected him and their priests declared, "We have no king but Caesar" (John 19:15). Another opportunity was missed.

God still wants his people to be a light to the nations by demonstrating his perfect system of government. Most Christians have rejected this challenge. They have refused God's system of justice and prefer to live under secular kings and democratic leaders. The nations do not understand the blessings of God's government, because there is no witness to its glory.

God Will Do It

Political philosophers have debated the ideal form of government since history began, but God settled the argument long ago. The ideal system of government is God's law applied by local judges and protection by temporary military leaders. This system has never been tried, even by the Israelites, but that does not mean it will not work. God knows what he is doing, so we can expect his social system to work better than any alternative.

The Holy Spirit will establish the Government of God on earth, but it will be different from what people expect. Peace will come when justice is administered by local judges applying God's Law and society is protected by temporary military leaders.

Christians have never taken God's system of government seriously. They have rejected God's law, and chosen democracy. As the Kingdom of God advances, human governments will fall away and be replaced with the perfect system of government that God revealed to Moses. The main purpose of this book is to explain how that would work.

4
Transforming Society

Bottom-up Society

Hierarchies of power pervade all the institutions of the modern world. Societies are structured from the top down. Authority flows down from the central government at the top. Political leaders decide how much power will be delegated to the regional and local authorities that control the structure of cities and towns.

Unfortunately, the perfect system of government that God gave to Moses will not work in a top-down, hierarchical society.

God was able to give a new model of government to the children of Israel, because they had left hierarchical controls behind when they escaped from Egypt. Their new society in the Promised Land was structured the other way round, with authority flowing from the bottom to the top. The greatest authority resided at the bottom among families and households, with only limited authority being delegated up.

This unique social structure was perfect for the government of God. In the next few sections, I will describe how it was intended to work and how it was later destroyed when the Israelites rejected God's government to be like other nations.

Before the Government of God can come to fullness in our time, modern society will need to be changed, so that authority flows from the bottom to the top. In the last part of this chapter, I will explain how the Holy Spirit can transform the followers of Jesus into local communities where God's perfect system of government can be established.

The Government of God is based on Free Authority, so it cannot be imposed from the top. The big challenge that I take on in this book is explaining how a human society can function effectively without hierarchy and control.

New Social Pattern

God's pattern for society was demonstrated when Moses led the children of Israel into the Promised Land. Up until then, God had worked through the families of people like Noah, Abraham and Jacob. He was now beginning a new stage of history with a nation of families, so he needed a suitable government.

While living in Egypt, the Israelites were controlled by slave masters exercising authority delegated down from Pharaoh. They did not need a political system because they had no authority. Their taskmasters controlled everything (Ex 1:11-13) and the leaders of families were powerless.

God could start with a clean slate in a new land, because Israel had no government hierarchy to be removed. Once they escaped from slavery, all that remained was their family connections. Families naturally linked up with other families from the same clan and tribe, because they knew and trusted them.

During the Exodus, the Israelites had no central authority, like the Pharaoh in Egypt. Moses was not a ruler, but a temporary military leader with very limited authority. He was an expert on life in the desert, because he had been a shepherd for forty years, but he could not force the people to do his will. If the leaders of families and tribes refused to follow his lead, he was powerless.

Joshua took over from Moses as temporary military leader, but when he died, God did not appoint a replacement. The main battle was over, so a national leader was not needed anymore. This seems strange to modern eyes, but God's system of government does not need a national leader.

Moses did not understand what God was doing, because he had been raised in the house of Pharaoh close to the centre of power. He had been trained by Pharaoh's courtiers, so he assumed that he would have to control the people from the top in the same way as Pharaoh controlled the Egyptians. Moses only realised that God was creating a new society with a different structure when he visited his father-in-law in the wilderness.

Jethro saw the strain that Moses was under because he was trying to be a national leader controlling everything. Jethro was a prophet, so he told Moses to give authority back to the leadership that already existed in the community and focus on representing the people before God (Ex 18:19).

The timing of Jethro's challenge was critical, because it came just before the Israelites would receive the law at Mount Sinai (Ex 19). While they were journeying to a new land, they needed a military leader to keep them safe, but God did not want this structure to continue into the Promised Land.

They Government of God cannot be established by Imposed Authority. The new system of law he was giving does not work in a top-down society, so God had to take authority away from Moses and give it back to the people.

Tens Fifties Hundreds Thousands

Jethro explained that authority should be restored to the people of the community who were already respected within their families.

> You shall look among the community for people who fear God, love the truth and hate corruption, and put them as heads of thousands, hundreds, fifties and tens (Exodus 18:21).

Moses did not appoint these people, because appointing a leader for every family in Israel would have stressed him even more. He did not know everyone personally, so he could not identify capable leaders who feared God. Instead, he placed authority back with families and households where God wanted it to be.

This society established in the new land would be based on families and households. Authority was pushed down to the lowest level of society. Relationships between families would determine its strength and shape.

Families could delegate authority up to leaders of Fifties, Hundreds and Thousands. They could decide who to trust and limit the authority they would give to them. The leaders of Fifties, Hundreds and Thousands were servants of those who gave them authority. They could not impose their will on them (Ex 18:23).

Moses could have chosen fancy names for the various groupings of society. Instead, he used the number of adults belonging to each group. For simplicity, I will continue this practice and refer to tens, fifties, hundreds and thousands. They are described more fully in the following sections.

Tens

The Ten was a broader concept than the modern nuclear family. It was a household consisting of two or three generations of the same family. The Hebrew expression for household is "bet ab", which literally means "fathers house". It usually included a father and mother, their adult sons and their wives, and their children. Jacob and his twelve adult sons together with their wives and children were a Ten when they went down to Egypt.

Elderly grandparents, unmarried aunts and uncles, widows and orphans could also belong to a Ten. Abraham included his nephew Lot in his household. Many households would include servants as well.

Ten is not the number of people in the household, but the number of men in the group capable of contributing to their protection. A Ten was a family or household that could release ten adult men to serve their community.

While wandering in the wilderness, a Ten was a household marching and camping together in close proximity. They would usually be linked by family ties, but they would also be united by a commitment to support and protect each other.

In the Promised Land, a Ten was a household working the plot of land that had been allocated to their family by ballot (Jos 14:1-5; Num 26:52-56). The leaders of tribes did not control the land. God's law ensured that each household kept their inheritance in the land (Lev 25:8-54; Num 27:8-11).

The household would live in several houses clustered together on their land or in a nearby village. These adjoining houses often shared one or more walls and a common courtyard for household tasks and cooking.

Each household was a cohesive economic unit, working their land together to provide food, clothing and shelter for each other. As a household grew in size, other activities might be developed to support the Ten.

Leader of the Ten

The leader of a Ten was usually the most senior person in the family, but another person might be recognised as leader, if they showed greater wisdom. Leaders of Tens exercised Free Authority, because participation in a Ten was voluntary. If the members of the Ten did not like what the leader is doing, they could switch their allegiance to a different person.

The leader of a Ten was responsible for negotiating with other Tens to form a Fifty or Hundred for a specific purpose. The members would only trust their leader's commitments, if they had been reliable in the past.

The Role of the Ten

The Household or Ten was the basic social unit in the Promised Land. It had several important functions.

- **Protection** – the men of a Ten joined together to protect their families.
- **Food** – the members of the Ten shared the food they gathered.
- **Welfare** – the members of the Ten shared their financial resources.
- **Resolving Disputes** – Most issues would be resolved within the family.
- **Employment** – The Ten provided employment for all its members.
- **Education** – the Ten would assist with educating each other's children.

The Bible never refers to Ten Commandments, but uses the expression "Ten Words" in three different places to describe the words of the covenant written on the tablets of stone.

> Moses wrote on the tablets the words of the covenant—
> the **Ten Words** (Ex 34:28).

The reference is not to the number of commands, but to the people who would use them most. Perhaps the statement should be translated as follows.

> Moses wrote on the tablets the words of the covenant—
> the **Words for Tens**.

God's covenant was a covenant with the entire community, but the commandments written on stone were his covenant with the Tens. They would be implemented by the Tens, so the Ten Commandments are really **Words for Tens**.

Fifties and Hundreds

The resources and capabilities of a household would be too limited to deal with some challenges. Several Tens might need to come together to deal with serious threats to their community. If all of the adults from four or five Tens came together for a specific purpose, they would be a Fifty. If a dozen Tens got together, they might be a Hundred. Fifties and Hundreds had four main purposes.

- **Welfare** – Financial support would flow from one Ten to another via family links.
- **Justice** – Links between the Tens were important for resolving disputes between people.
- **Defence** –several Tens could come together to deal with an external threat.

Fifties and Hundred derived authority from the Tens within them. They could only act, if the leaders of the Tens gave permission.

Thousands

Several Hundreds could join together for a task needing more resources. The main purpose of a Thousand was defence. If the leaders of several Fifties and Hundreds agreed, they could raise a Thousand men to defend their community. The leaders of the hundreds would choose one person to be their leader.

The leaders of Thousands exercised Free Authority so they could only operate with the support of the participating groups. If they abused their authority, submission could be withdrawn and their authority would evaporate.

Thousands were voluntary and temporary. One would come together to deal with a threatening army and when they were defeated, they would return to their homes (Jos 22:6).

Kings destroy Tens Fifties and Hundreds

The social structure that Moses had given Israel did not last long. It was replaced by a system of kings copied from the surrounding nations (1 Sam 8). This was a shocking change, because kingship relies on Imposed Authority. Samuel warned of the danger.

> This is what the king who will reign over you will do: He will take your sons and make them serve with his chariots and horses, and they will run in front of his chariots. He will take your daughters to be perfumers and cooks and bakers (1 Sam 8 11,13).

The king would take young people to serve in his army and palace. At a critical time during their growth to maturity, when they would normally be developing a role in their community, the young person would be taken out for service to the king.

Loyalty to the king would replace their loyalty to their Ten, Fifty and Hundred. The leader of their Ten would lose their respect. Their relationships with other young people in the king's service would become stronger than their relationship with their Ten and Hundred. This undermined the structure of society.

Samuel warned that kings would bring back Imposed Authority.

> Some he will assign to be commanders of thousands and commanders of fifties (1 Sam 8:12).

The king would appoint loyal followers to be commanders over thousands and fifties. This was a radical change.

Under the system established by Moses, the leader of a Fifty or Hundred was chosen by the members of the Tens who joined it. The leader of a Thousand was selected by the leaders of the

Hundreds, who agreed to participate for a purpose. Leadership emerged from the bottom and submission was voluntary.

Kingship turned this model on its head. Instead of leaders emerging from within, they would be appointed from outside by the king. The members of a Fifty or Thousand had to submit to the king's man, even if he made foolish decisions. Refusal to obey the king's lapdog would bring down the wrath of the king.

Under the kingship, the Thousand stopped being a temporary and voluntary force and became a permanent tool for imposing the king's control over society. Free Authority rising from the bottom was replaced by Imposed Authority from the top. The people lost their freedom and came under the control of the king.

Justice disappeared when kings took control of legal disputes. King's justice protected those with wealth and connection (2 Sam 15:2-4).

Modern Society

Industrialisation, globalisation, migration and urbanisation have fragmented the structure of modern society leaving individuals and families isolated from each other. This breakdown is greatest in modern cities, where social mobility has destroyed family and community relationships. Modern life is characterised by separation and personal insecurity.

Modern suburban culture creates barriers to communication and encourages individualism. People drive in and out of the suburb for work, shopping and recreation, but rarely meet with each other. As communities weaken and fear increases, high fences go up between houses isolating people from each other.

Social isolation means that most people do not belong to the community where they live. Unfortunately, Christians are almost as socially fragmented as the rest of society.

The fragmentation of society makes Imposed Authority seem like the only solution. The isolation and dislocation of urban society has been paralleled by the accumulation of political power in the modern state.

To restore the cohesion of our communities and societies, Tens, Fifties and Hundreds need to be restored. Jesus showed how it could happen by restoring Tens and Hundreds in his time.

Tens Fifties and Hundreds Restored

Jesus began his ministry by forming a Ten.

> Jesus went up on a mountainside and called to him those he wanted, and they came to him. He appointed **twelve**—designating them apostles—that they might be with him. These are the twelve he appointed (Mark 3:13-16).

When Jesus fed the five thousand, he put them people in Fifties and Hundreds. This was a prophetic act.

> They sat down in groups of **hundreds and fifties** (Mark 6:40).

By the time of Pentecost, the new church had become a Hundred.

> They all joined together constantly in prayer, along with the women and Mary the mother of Jesus, and with his brothers. In those days Peter stood up among the believers (a group numbering about a **hundred and twenty**) (Acts 1:14-15).

As the church expanded, they continued to share in Tens, Fifties and Hundreds.

> Every day they continued to meet together in the temple courts. They broke bread in their homes and ate together with glad and sincere hearts (Acts 2:46).

The early church undertook most of the roles that had been undertaken by Tens, Fifties and Hundreds in Moses' time.

1. **Welfare** – the church supported people who fell into poverty. The Christians who met together in homes also shared their financial resources.

> Selling their possessions and goods, they gave to anyone as he had need (Acts 2:45).

2. **Protection** – the church provided protection for their community. The religious and political leaders in Jerusalem were hostile to the new movement that emerged, but the Christians protected themselves by sticking together.

> All the believers were together (Acts 2:44).

While they were together, the authorities could not touch them.

3. **Justice** – the new movement implemented biblical justice. The Book of Acts says there were "no needy persons among them" (Acts 4:34). The Greek word translated as "needy" is "endees". It is not the usual word for "poverty" and is only used once in the New Testament. It is a compound of the word "bind". Luke is saying that no one among them was "bound by injustice".

These early Christians were not in a position to achieve legal solutions to the individual injustices that had left some people destitute and others wealthy. They resolved them with overwhelming generosity instead.

Many of the new Christians sold property and gave it away (Acts 4:34). Luke did not use the normal word for "inheritance". This suggests that the early Christians were not giving away their inheritances; they were giving away property that they had acquired unjustly as a way of making restitution.

Tens Fifties and Hundreds Again

A church that extracts new Christians from their network of worldly relationships and gathers them in a meeting hidden in a building far from home and work is not going to change the world. If we want to change the world, we will need to get back into our neighbourhoods and establish real community.

The gospel should restore Tens, Fifties and Hundreds. In my book Being Church Where We Live, I described how a group of people following Jesus can become a community within their neighbourhood. They would be led by four or five elders, each with a different gifting, but submitted to each other for unity. Each elder would provide oversight for about five or six families.

If all the families overseen by an elder lived in close proximity, they would be able to fulfil all the functions of a Ten. If the neighbourhood church had about five elders, each providing oversight of a Ten, the entire group would be a Fifty. A couple of neighbourhood churches working together would be a Hundred.

By living in the same location, they could parallel the experience of the Israelite families and households who settled in the Promised Land. Instead of being linked by kinship, they would be linked by love for one another. A community based on commitment to Jesus would be stronger than one based on family connections, because it would have more diverse giftings.

If the members of neighbourhood churches operated as Tens, Fifties or Hundreds in the place where they have chosen to live, cohesiveness would be restored to their community. However, this can only happen if we get out of our cars and auditoriums and choose to live closer to each other.

Tens and Fifties will be shaped by the "one another stuff". Their leaders will not control the people they are watching over, but will serve them. Elders will exercise Free Authority, so no one will be forced to do what they do not want to do.

Thousands

The resources and capabilities of a Fifty or Hundred might be insufficient to deal with a serious problem. When faced by an external threat, a number of neighbourhood churches might work together on a common defence. This is the main role of the Thousand. I will explain how it could work in chapters 13-14.

A Thousand derives its functions and authority from below. Its leaders only have authority, if the elders of the neighbourhood churches freely agree to submit to them. They can with draw that submission at any time.

Authority Shift

Tens and Fifties will serve everyone in the neighbourhood, including those who have rejected the gospel. Their love will draw people who are not committed to Jesus into their activities, especially those that provide justice, welfare and protection.

To benefit from the activities of a Ten or Fifty, they will have to compromise their behaviour to fit in with the lifestyle of the followers of Jesus. However, no one will be forced to change. They will be free to opt out of community activities whenever they choose.

Authority in the neighbourhood will shift toward Jesus.

- Tens and Fifties will be the most influential groups in their neighbourhood.

- The Tens will be serving Jesus.
- They will have freely submitted to the Free Authority of their elders.
- The elders will be submitted to Jesus and to each other.
- People living in the neighbourhood but not following Jesus will submit to elders when they participate in the activities of a Ten or Fifty.
- The spiritual powers of evil will be squeezed out of the neighbourhood, because there is no Imposed Authority amplifying their power.

Taken together, this means that most people in the neighbourhood will be submitted to God at least some of the time, so the Kingdom of God has come. Each Fifty will be a Kingdom Community.

5

Kingdom Communities

Territory

A king needs territory. A kingdom is a geographic area or territory controlled by the king. The boundary of a kingdom was never fixed, so most kings tried to expand their authority by pushing out the boundary of their kingdom. A king who was not expanding his kingdom was perceived to be weak.

A king usually ruled from a castle or palace at the centre of his kingdom. He could expand his territory by pushing out from this stronghold into places where a neighbouring king was vulnerable. Once he has taken the new territory, the king would build defences and put his own army in place to protect it. By constantly pushing out and seizing more territory, a strong king could expand his kingdom.

The castle was a safe place where the king could retreat if he suffered a setback in battle. Another king might seize some of his territory, but would struggle to conquer the stronghold at the centre of the kingdom. The defeated king would retreat to his castle and rejuvenate his army ready to push out and regain the territory that has been lost.

If the king hid in his castle and didn't try to retake the territory that the enemy king had stolen, his kingdom would shrink and eventually disappear. Any loyal citizens living in the lost territory would be robbed and beaten by enemy soldiers. Even if they went to the castle once a week to honour their king, they would eventually get tired of being harassed and begrudgingly accept the authority of the enemy king who dominated their lives.

Jesus Needs Territory

Most Christians have failed to understand the importance of territory for the spiritual struggle we are engaged in. Whereas the early Christians were "together in one place", we have scattered ourselves in houses far from each other. We go to church once a week to honour Jesus, but have not bothered to establish evil-spirit-free places where Jesus' authority is recognised.

The spiritual powers of evil understand the importance of territory. The powerful ones have become "principalities and powers" controlling nations and kingdoms by dominating the kings and political leaders with authority over them. Lesser spirits control small areas where they have been given authority.

Jesus now has many followers in the world, but very little territory where he has authority. There are very few places where he is king. Instead, his followers are scattered throughout territory that is controlled by the enemy. Because we live and work in enemy territory, we are often battered, beaten and robbed.

A king without a territory is not a real king. He is just a dreamer. If there are no areas on earth that are evil-spirit free, then Jesus does not have a kingdom on earth. He just has people living in enemy territory, who have given allegiance to him. This should disturb us. Jesus needs followers who understand the importance of territory.

Clearing Territory

The Kingdom of God expands as Jesus' followers push the spiritual powers of evil out of territory and bring it under his authority. Once the importance of territory is understood, the keys to a successful strategy become clear.

- ***Victory comes through many small steps.***
  A wise king seizes control of a piece of a territory and consolidates his authority there, before advancing to take

the next piece. When the Israelites entered the Promised Land, God undertook to drive out their enemy "little by little" (Deut 7:22). The Kingdom of God advances in the same way. We must take back territory for Jesus, house by house and neighbourhood by neighbourhood. Once a piece of territory is safe, we can push out into the neighbouring territory, resisting the enemy powers as we go.

- *Attack where the enemy is vulnerable*
  People resisting an evil king will usually gather in a quiet place on the edge of the kingdom, where the king's position is weak. Jesus did not go straight to Jerusalem. He began his ministry in Galilee, where he could move about freely without being noticed by the Jewish leaders and Roman governors colluding together to control the country. He only went to Jerusalem to confront the religious and political authorities at the end of his ministry.

  Christians starting something new often go to the centre of the city where the need is greatest. This is a mistake, because the spiritual powers of evil are strongest at the centre of the city, where they conspire with the governing authorities. We cannot defeat a big principality that controls a city or nation all at once, but we can push them back from the edges one small piece of territory at a time.

- *Concentrated force leads to victory.*
  A loyal citizen standing alone cannot establish a place where his king has authority, because he will be overwhelmed by the surrounding forces. A group of citizens gathered in one place can resist their enemy. When persecuted by Saul, David gathered a few distressed and disgruntled people in the Cave of Adullam. They became a great army that established David as King.

  Christians who live in the suburbs and drive to a church some distance from where they live will struggle to spiritually defend their homes, because they are standing alone. They cannot take territory, because the spiritual powers of evil can concentrate to attack them.

When people are led by the Spirit to live close together, they can stand against the attacks of the enemy and establish a place where Jesus has authority. When a group of people who are united in love and empowered by the spirit live in the same place, they can take that territory for Jesus.

Implementing this strategy will require a different kind of church. Driving to a church meeting once a week will not be enough. God is calling his people to establish neighbourhood churches to win back territory. A neighbourhood church is a group of people living close together in the same location, loving one another and serving Jesus in the power of the Spirit.

Each neighbourhood church will be led by a team of elders with complementary gifts. They will be united by love for Jesus and each other. They will disciple those who have chosen to follow Jesus and build relationships between them.

Each neighbourhood church should be attached to a particular locality and there can be as many churches as there are different localities. Ideally, there should only be one church in each location and each location should have just one church.

Retaking Territory

Neighbourhood churches are the key to retaking territory for Jesus, so efforts to establish them will have to be quite deliberate. The next few sections describe one way this can be done. However, the Holy Spirit is creative and can do it in dozens of different ways, if his people listen to his voice.

The Holy Spirit will usually begin when a few friends who have learned to trust each other choose to do something new and better in a new place. They should have giftings that complement each other. One will be passionate about sharing the gospel, while another might be more visionary. At least one will have a shepherd's heart. Despite their differences, they will have learned to serve Jesus in unity.

The friends will move to a neighbourhood where the Holy Spirit is working. Ideally, they will know someone living in the neighbourhood who is open to the gospel and has many friends there. This is the person of peace described by Jesus (Luke 10:6).

- To avoid conflict and unnecessary confusion, they should go to a neighbourhood where other churches are inactive.
- The spiritual pressure in a city is not evenly distributed, so the battle is tougher close to political power at the centre. The best place to start will be at the edge of the city where spiritual opposition is weaker.
- Establishing a beachhead in a strategic locality and then expanding outward is a very effective way to take a city. An army takes a city street by street and neighbourhood by neighbourhood.
- Christians are tempted to work in the centre of the city, but it is the toughest place to work. Advancing from a stronghold at the edge will be more successful.
- The spiritual powers of evil concentrate on powerful people at the centre of the culture, so they can leverage their power. They neglect those at the edges, because they are already distressed and broken.
- People in more distressed places will be more open to the gospel, because they know they are needy.
- God begins building his Kingdom on the fringe of society, where it will not attract attention and opposition. When the power at the centre folds and fails, his Kingdom will expand from the edges.
- People who live outside the neighbourhood should be excluded, except for prayer. Anyone who wants to be part of the new body must come and live in the neighbourhood. Christians who are not sufficiently committed to move to where God is moving will be a distraction and a hindrance.

In this context, a neighbourhood is not a large suburb, but a street, a block or cluster of houses. The people sharing in a neighbourhood church must live within walking distance of each other, so they can share their resources and serve each together. They will not be the only people in the locality, but will leave room for others to live amongst them and watch how they live.

Elders

Once the neighbourhood church starts to grow, new believers will recognise the people who moved into the street as elders. They will teach them how to listen to the Holy Spirit and follow Jesus.

One of the elders will watch over each Christian living in the neighbourhood, but they will not be heavy-handed. They will mostly just pray for them. The elders will ensure that everyone in the neighbourhood church is growing into their ministry.

The elders will be committed to unity. When making a decision that could affect the advance of the gospel, they will always check with each other, before taking action. When division comes into the body, they will act to restore peace and unity.

The elders will be committed to loving and serving everyone in their neighbourhood. They will be welcome everywhere, because they do good to those in need, but do not impose their standards on those they bless.

A neighbourhood church is a network of relationships between people living close together and watched over by a team of elders who are united in love for Jesus.

Spiritual Stronghold

Territory is critical to the Government of God. God has given humans authority on earth, so he needs places where people have given him permission to work. Like other kings, he establishes a stronghold of safety and pushes out into new territory.

To defeat the spiritual powers of evil, God needs places where his people have given the Holy Spirit full freedom to operate. A single house or a church building does not give him much scope. The Holy Spirit will be more effective, if his followers establish a stronghold in a group of dwellings close to each other.

The best way to take territory for Jesus is a group of his followers living close together in one place. Living in unity in the same place expands their spiritual authority, because Jesus promises to be there with them.

> For where two or three gather in my name, there am I with
> them (Matt 18:20).

They have authority in their homes. By standing together, they have authority to force the spiritual powers of evil to leave the vicinity of their homes.

A small group of believers living at the same location, united by love and submitted to Jesus can resist the spiritual powers of evil and force them to flee some territory.

> Whatever you bind on earth will be bound in the spiritual realms (Mat 18:18).

When three or four families who are united by their love of Jesus and empowered by the Spirit move to a place and live close to each other, they can drive out the spiritual powers of evil that control it. If one family had moved on their own, they would struggle, because the powers of evil could concentrate to pick them off.

If the people living in a cluster of dwellings follow Jesus and stand together against the spiritual powers of evil, they can establish an evil spirit-free zone where the Holy Spirit is free to work and a neighbourhood church can emerge. The people in the six darker shaded houses have chosen to follow Jesus. The lightly shaded area is an evil-spirit-free zone, where the Holy Spirit can operate freely.

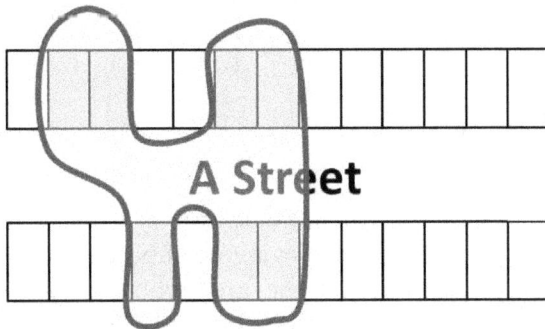

Unlike other kings, God will not expand his territory using force to gain control of people (He will only use force against the spiritual powers of evil). His influence increases as his people:

- force the spiritual powers of evil out of the surrounding neighbourhood.

- love and serve the people they live amongst.
- share the good news of Jesus and his new government.
- teach those who accept the good news to listen to the Holy Spirit and follow Jesus.

Once a spiritual stronghold has been established, the Holy Spirit will be able to move freely. When the friends share their faith, the Holy Spirit will confirm their words with gifts of healing. Everyone will see what is happening and some will choose to follow Jesus.

Each new believer will be taught to do Jesus' will by listening to the Holy Spirit. Before long, they will be sharing the gospel in the power of the Spirit with their neighbours and friends.

As more people choose to follow Jesus, the spiritual stronghold will expand in the neighbourhood and the intensity of the Holy Spirit's presence will increase. Healings will be more frequent and the gospel will be more effective. As more people choose to follow Jesus, a new neighbourhood church will emerge and the territory under his authority will grow.

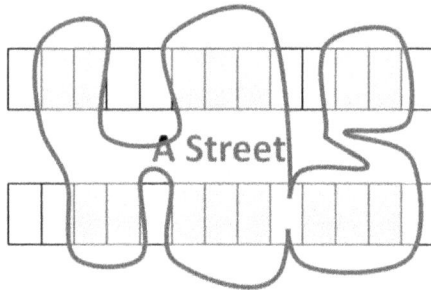

When residents of the surrounding houses choose to follow Jesus, they can join with their believing neighbours to squeeze the spiritual powers of evil out of the area where they live. The territory where Holy Spirit is free to work expands and the authority of Jesus grows.

Jesus needs teams of followers who understand the importance of territory. By living close together, they can work with the Holy Spirit to drive the spiritual powers of evil out of the area where they live.

Apostolic Team

When the neighbourhood church has grown to about forty adults and their families, the elders will prepare to move out and start again. An apostolic team will be sent to a place where followers of Jesus are already having an impact on their neighbours. The following principles should apply to an apostolic team.

- The best people must be sent out to start the new work. This will include some of the people who started the original neighbourhood church.
- The elders will have identified people with potential to be elders and spent time with them, so they can take over when they are ready to leave.
- The apostolic team should not go far, because they will want to maintain relationships with the neighbourhood church they are leaving.
- They should go and live in the new place, so their commitment to it is visible.
- The apostolic team will go where the Holy Spirit is working.
- If the Holy Spirit is leading the apostolic team, their number will grow quickly. In a very short time, they will have grown into a neighbourhood church.

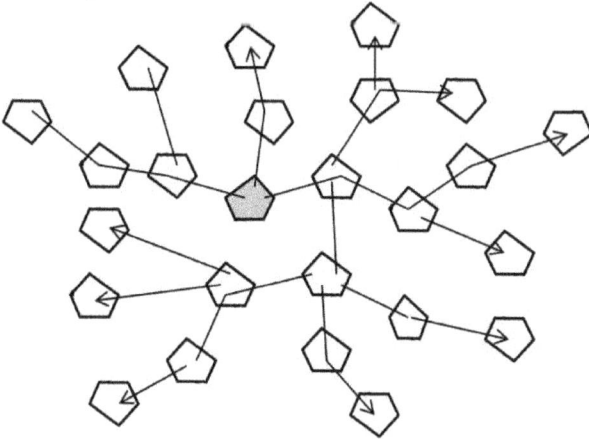

This apostolic approach can be applied and repeated anywhere. If the Holy Spirit is moving powerfully, most neighbourhood churches will quickly get to a point where they can send out an apostolic team to start again in a new locality. After several years, some apostolic teams will have moved on three or four times and established new neighbourhood churches in several places.

Establishing a beachhead in a strategic locality and then expanding outward is a very effective way to take control of territory. As neighbourhood churches expand and multiply, the territory where Jesus is acknowledged as king will expand.

Kingdom Communities

Each neighbourhood church consisted of a group of forty or fifty adults following Jesus together in the same location, but that is not the ultimate goal. For the Kingdom of God to come, neighbourhood churches must be transformed into Kingdom Communities that can reshape their neighbourhood.

Modern societies are shaped and controlled from the centre by human government. When human governments collapse, the situation will be ripe for the Holy Spirit to do something special. Social and civic services will shrink, and people who depend on them will find themselves in dire circumstances.

Neighbourhood churches will fill the gap by taking over all the roles currently undertaken by human governments. Everything that the human government is failing to do, the neighbourhood church will do better, but without force or coercion. When the neighbourhood church has replaced the human government in their neighbourhood, it has become a Kingdom Community.

Modern human governments have taken on four main roles: social support, justice, protection and defence. They do none of these well. As human governments struggle under the stress of traumatic events, neighbourhood churches will step up and take responsibility for these tasks, but in a totally different way.

Neighbourhood churches will already have been providing financial support and physical protection for followers of Jesus. Elders will have been resolving disputes between the people they are watching over. A neighbourhood church becomes a Kingdom Community when these services are offered to the rest of the community, but without using Imposed Authority.

A Kingdom Community will provide financial support, justice and protection for everyone living in the community. People who have not accepted the gospel will let the elders of the neighbourhood church serve them. They will often accept their authority because they recognise their love and integrity.

Neighbourhood churches should prepare for the future by transforming into Kingdom Communities.

1. Welfare
Modern governments are deeply entwined in the economies they control. When they collapse, economies will be devastated. People who depend on government welfare will find that their economic support is gone.

Followers of Jesus will have lived simply, so a neighbourhood church should have spare resources. They will commit to serving everyone in their street facing financial difficulty. The neighbourhood church will provide financial support to everyone in need, even those who have rejected Jesus. Providing support for people who were hostile to their message will be a tremendous witness (more in Chapter 12).

2. Justice
Theft and violence hurt people and undermine the cohesiveness of a society. Local judges applying God's laws against theft and violence are the best solution.

Participants in a neighbourhood church will take their disputes to their elders. If one demonstrates a gift of wisdom, the other elders will refer difficult cases to them. Residents within the community will bring their disputes to this elder.

When reports of the elder's wisdom spread, they will gain credibility beyond their community. More and more people will bring disputes to them. The elder will be recognised as a judge, as people discover their wisdom and bring disputes for resolution.

Elders in a Kingdom Community can only offer voluntary justice, because they do not have legal authority to enforce their decisions. Their authority comes from the respect that they have in their neighbourhood. (More on justice in Chapters 6-10).

3. Physical Protection

The neighbourhood church will take responsibility for keeping the people safe for protecting their neighbourhood from attack. They will provide protection for everyone, including those who have rejected the gospel.

If dangerous people come into the neighbourhood, they will be noticed quickly, because everyone will know each other. The people of the community will gather to pray. Others will talk with the intruders and offer them food and help. When the intruders see the unity of the people, they will usually go off to look for easier pickings (See Chapter 13 for more on protection).

Other Needs

The Kingdom Community will take up other tasks that are currently seen as the responsibility of the government. As human government collapses, the followers of Jesus will endeavour to meet all needs that emerge in their neighbourhood. They will take responsibility for education, sanitation, rubbish collection, road maintenance, etc. Some of these roles will be done by new businesses that emerge in the community.

Meeting the needs of so many people will be costly, but giving for the service of others is normal for the followers of Jesus. It is another way of taking up the cross to follow Jesus.

As the neighbourhood church freely provides more and more of the services that were previously provided by the civil government, everyone in the neighbourhood will be influenced. The leadership of the elders organising these services will be recognised by everyone in their neighbourhood. People who have rejected the gospel will acknowledge their wisdom, because they are dedicated to serving their community.

Citizens and Residents

A kingdom is a territory where a king exercises authority. Two categories of people live within the territory of a kingdom.

- **Citizens** are loyal to their king and will fight for him when he calls for their help. They have pledged their allegiance to the king and are keen to obey his decrees.

- **Residents** live within the kingdom (temporally or permanently) but they are not loyal to the king. To keep out of trouble, they will grudgingly accept the king's authority, because he is the dominant power in the territory. Residents will not fight for the king, if they can avoid it. If they get a chance, they might even undermine him. Most will keep their heads down so they can go about their lives without being caught up in the power struggles of kings.

David was resident in Saul's kingdom, but his allegiance was to God. Shimei the son of Gera was a resident of David's kingdom, but he was not a citizen, because he remained loyal to Saul (2 Sam 16:5-14). Ziba the steward of Mephibosheth was a citizen, because he remained loyal even when David was being pushed out of his kingdom (2 Sam 16:1-4).

In the same way, two categories of people live within a Kingdom Community.

- **Citizens of a Kingdom Community** have freely submitted to Jesus by listening to the Holy Spirit and obeying his word.
- **Residents of a Kingdom Community** live within the neighbourhood, but they have not accepted the gospel or chosen to follow Jesus. They may want to receive the blessings that flow from participation in the Kingdom Community, but they are not full citizens, because they have chosen not to surrender to Jesus.

Citizens will support the work of the Spirit by loving and sharing with the residents of their neighbourhood. They will provide justice, support and protection for anyone with a need, free of charge and control. However, residents will have to acknowledge the authority of the elders of the neighbourhood church to receive these benefits.

Participation in the activities of a Kingdom Community will always be voluntary. However, when residents freely submit to the elders to obtain the benefits provided, they will be submitting to the authority of Jesus, even if they have not acknowledged him as their Lord.

Jesus' Territory

A Kingdom Community will become territory where most of the people freely submit to the authority of Jesus, either as citizens or residents.

- Followers of Jesus will be united against the spiritual powers of evil and push them out of the neighbourhood.
- As the human government weakens and withdraws, the authority of the kingdom of man will decline.
- As political power declines, the spiritual powers of evil will lose their grip and become easier to defeat.
- The neighbourhood church will expand its influence by meeting the needs of everyone previously supported by collapsing human governments.
- Most people in the neighbourhood will rely on the justice, protection and financial support provided by the neighbourhood church, even if they have rejected the gospel.
- Residents of the Kingdom Community will have to acknowledge the authority of the elders who are serving their needs.
- The elders of the neighbourhood church will not seize control, but serve their community, so that people freely accept their leading.
- The elders exercise Free Authority, received when people freely submit to their wisdom, but this submission can be withdrawn at any time.
- No one will be forced to submit to the authority of the elders. There is no room for Imposed Authority in a Kingdom Community.
- Most of the authority in the neighbourhood will disappear or be submitted to Jesus.
- As respect for Jesus spreads through the community, more and more of the authority that shapes society will be submitted to him.

The territory that belongs to Jesus will expand as the authority situation in the neighbourhood changes.

- Citizens of the Kingdom Community will freely submit to the authority of their elders, to each other, and to God.
- The elders will have submitted to Jesus, and to each other.
- Residents within the Kingdom Community will submit to God's authority most of the time to benefit from the activities of the neighbourhood church.
- The number of people refusing to submit to the leading of the Spirit will steadily decrease as the gospel spreads and the benefits of the good news are realised.

Taken together, this means that many of the people in the neighbourhood are submitted to God's will most of the time, and most for much of the time. The Government of God has come, because his will is being done within the territory covered by the Kingdom Community.

Yeast

Society cannot be transformed from the top down by changing the government. The Government of God will emerge as Kingdom Communities transform society by spreading out from neighbourhood to neighbourhood, like yeast in kneaded dough.

> He told them still another parable: "The kingdom of heaven is like yeast that a woman took and mixed into about sixty pounds of flour until it worked all through the dough" (Matt 13:33).

The yeast is almost invisible, but as the woman kneads the flour, it spreads through the dough and transforms it into bread. The Kingdom of God gradually spreads throughout society like yeast hidden in flour.

The first Kingdom Communities will be hidden in isolated places that no one cares about. God does not work in the centres of power, but on the margins of society where worldly wisdom does not go. Because Imposed Authority is avoided, most people will not even realise that a new government is emerging.

The more the dough is kneaded, the more the yeast will spread. During tough times when everyone is struggling, Kingdom Communities will grow stronger and stronger.

When the political, business, religious and spiritual powers entwined together at the centre collapse, Kingdom Communities that have been invisible on the edge of society will multiply and grow. God's invisible kingdom will spread out from community to community and neighbourhood to neighbourhood.

Each new Kingdom Community will be a beachhead from which it can be launched into the next neighbourhood. The good news will spread from house to house. An entire society can be transformed, person by person, household by household, locality by locality.

Kingdom Communities will multiply and grow. As they push out the spiritual powers of evil, the territory that is loyal to Jesus will be enlarged.

6
Perfect Law

Law is Good

If every person in the world was like Jesus, people everywhere could live in harmony without tension. Unfortunately, sin is pervasive. When humans live close to each other, they hurt other people, or take things that others have worked hard to get. Some people will always be tempted by theft and violence.

Law provides a powerful solution to these problems, but laws only work, if they are implemented promptly and fairly, so every society with good laws needs good judges to apply them. This leads to two basic questions.

- Who should make the laws?
- Who will be the judges?

In the modern world, the laws are made by the government and judges are appointed by the government.

- Human governments have a monopoly on law-making.
- Government appointed judges have a monopoly on justice.

In a kingdom, the king makes the law, so in the Kingdom of God, God is the law-giver for his Kingdom.

> For the Lord is our judge,
> the Lord is our law-giver (Is 33:22).

The law will be God's law, and he will raise up judges to apply it.

Source of Law

Every society needs laws to function. There are two ways a society can get the law it needs.

- We can get our law from God.
- We can make up our own law.

Most modern nations have chosen the second option. They have a Parliament or a Congress to make the laws for the nation. Many Christians agree with this approach. They are happy to accept laws made by the parliament or congress in their nation. This is odd, because human laws will always be inferior to God's law.

God is the only person wise enough to be a law-giver. He has not delegated lawgiving to anyone else, so human lawmakers are usurping his authority. He has given his ideal law, so we do not need politicians to make laws.

Good Law

God's law is good. Paul confirmed this in his Roman letter.

> So then, the law is holy, and the commandment is holy, righteous and good... We know that the law is spiritual (Rom 7:12,14).

God's law is holy, righteous, spiritual and good. This is as good as law can be. Substituting man-made laws for laws that are holy and good is foolish.

Elected politicians and parliaments have limited knowledge, so they tend to produce inadequate laws. The best that they can do is add to God's law, but that is unwise. He warned that adding to his law is a serious mistake.

> Do not add to what I command you and do not subtract from it, but keep the commands of the Lord your God that I give you (Deut 4:1-2).

Two Laws

God's Laws for Society boil down to two simple laws.

- You shall not steal.
- You shall not assault a person with physical force.

The command against murder is a special case of the second law that applies when the person struck dies from their injuries. The remedy is different, but it is just a more serious form of assault.

Scope of Theft
Stealing is not limited to theft, but includes any careless action that harms another's property. These are described in the verdicts of the law.
- Breaking into a person's house and taking things (Ex 22:2);
- Finding something lost by another person and selling it (Deut 22 1-2);
- Borrowing something from another person and losing it (Ex 22:14);
- Damaging something that has been borrowed (Ex 22:14-15);
- Using another person's equipment without permission (Ex 22:10).
- Losing something entrusted for safekeeping (Ex 22:7).
- The seduction of a young woman (Ex 22:16).
- Allowing animals to wander and destroy another person's crop (Ex 22:5).
- Allowing fire to spread and destroy property (Ex 22:6).
- Fraud (Lev 19:13);
- Embezzlement (Lev 19:35);
- Breaking a contract to sell or buy at an agreed price (Ex 20:16);
- Actions that harm other people (Ex 23:5);
- Lying to a judge about another person (Deut 19:16-19).

Two questions help determine whether theft has occurred. Did the goods taken belong to someone else? Were the goods or service taken without their permission? Taking something that belongs to another person without their permission is forbidden.

Scope of Assault
Assault includes any action that causes harm to another person.
- Striking with the fist or weapon(Ex 21:18-19);
- Violence with intention to kill (Ex 21:14);
- Manslaughter (Ex 21:13);
- Assaulting a parent is particularly serious (Ex 21:15);
- Kidnapping (Ex 21:16);

- A curse that affects a person's body (Ex 21:17);
- Violence against an employee (Ex 21:20-21);
- An innocent bystander being injured by men fighting (Ex 21:22-25);
- Allowing an animal or machinery to hurt another person (Ex 21:28-32);
- Leaving a hazard unguarded that could hurt another person (Ex 21:33-36);
- Sexual seduction is a serious assault (Ex 22:16-17).

Benefits of God's Law
God's law has the following advantages.

1. Easy to Understand
I refer to God's laws as Laws for Society, because ordinary people can understand them. You do not have to be a lawyer to know what they mean. Every child knows what stealing means: "Billy has taken my book".

In some modern commercial situations, the nature of theft is harder to discern, but the issue is still the same. If the person did not pay for it, and the owner did not give it to them, it is stolen.

A very young child can understand that striking another person is wrong. "Billy hit me". Some assaults are more sophisticated, but the result is the same. A person receives an injury from another person using force against them.

God's law is easy for judges to apply. It is easy to understand, so judges do not need law degrees. What they need is wisdom to discern the truth (the judge's role is described in chapter 8).

2. Universal Laws
A law can only work if it is widely accepted. If too many people disagree with a law, it will be ignored. If people hate enough laws, they will become hostile to the law-maker.

God's Laws for Society are accepted everywhere. In every society, except those that are very evil, assault is recognised as wrong. Likewise, theft is usually seen as wrong. Most societies already have laws against theft and assault. God's two laws have already been accepted almost everywhere.

People know that stealing and assault are wrong, because we are created in God's image, and his laws are written on our hearts. People might repress their consciences with respect to their own behaviour, but they still believe these things are wrong for other people. These are universal laws.

3. Timeless laws

God's two laws are timeless. The things that are stolen change over time, but the nature of stealing remains the same. In Moses' time, a sheep or oxen might be stolen. Today it is more likely to be a car or a phone, but the effect is the same. Someone takes something that does not belong to them.

The method used to commit an assault has changed, but the consequences remain the same. In Moses' time, people threw rocks, whereas these days, they might use a knife or a gun. The only difference is that the injuries inflicted might be more severe and death more common.

4. Humble Law

God's Laws for Society are perfect for their purpose. Someone living within a community of people can hurt their neighbour in two main ways.

- They can take something that belongs to the neighbour. This is covered by God's first Law for Society.
- They can hurt their neighbour's physical body. God's second Law for Society deals with this situation.

God's laws are designed to allow a community of people to live together in close proximity. It deals with the two main ways that neighbours can hurt each other. By providing a way to deal with this harm, laws support the development of a strong community.

The Laws for Society does not try to do too much, because they recognise the limits of what can be done, if hearts are not changed. Often the best that God's law can achieve is to minimise theft and violence. That is not much, but it is enough for a society to live in relative harmony.

Human law always tries to do more. It is expected to solve every problem: eliminate poverty, eradicate racism, transform the economy, save the environment, and all before lunch. Human law tries to do everything, but succeeds at nothing. Worst of all, it fails at restraining theft and violence. Law and more always fails.

5. Law Releases Blessings
Wonderful blessings flow from God's law.

> All these blessings will come on you and accompany you if you obey the Lord your God. You will be blessed in the city and blessed in the country (Deut 28:2-3).

The two Laws for Society release economic blessing. People will not work hard to produce an economic surplus, if they fear it will be stolen the moment they turn their back. They will not create capital equipment if they are scared that someone will threaten them and take it. By placing a constraint on theft and violence, people are free to be productive and build their capital. By selling what they have produced, the entire society benefits.

6. Limited Authority
The Laws for Society do not attempt to deal with all sin. A sin is an act that is contrary to the commands of God. A law is a command of God that is punishable by judges.   Laws deal with only a few sins. Every law has two parts.

- An action is forbidden. The law must be precise enough for anyone to understand what is prohibited.
- A penalty is specified for non-compliance. Those who break a law receive a negative sanction or punishment. A law without sanction is just a suggestion.

Specifying a penalty authorises judges to deal with a sin. Greed might be morally wrong, but no punishment is specified for being greedy, so judges cannot do anything about it.

Laws can be identified by determining whether a punishment is specified. If there is no sanction, a sin is not unlawful. Judges have no authority to deal with a sin with no sanctions specified. This places a clear limit on the authority of judges.

God's law does not attempt to control sinful thoughts and attitudes, as law can only deal with actions. He can see into people's hearts, so he is the only one who can deal with most other sins. He has kept that responsibility for himself.

7. Fostering Freedom

Good laws foster freedom, by specificying actions that are forbidden. This negative phrasing means that judges have no authority until a crime has occurred. This seems odd, but an example will explain.

You shall not steal.

The negative wording means that this law only effects those who steal. It places no demands on anyone who does not steal, so they are free to do what they like with their money. A negative law has no relevance for those who do not break it.

A positively stated law would give judges unlimited power. Consider a positively stated version of the same law.

You must spend your money wisely.

This law would give judges the right to monitor and challenge every financial transaction. Judges would have authority to check on every person who spends money. This would be extremely dangerous and people would lose their freedom.

8. Not System of Rules

Human legislatures produce complex systems of rules, but they fail because they cannot deal with every possible situation. No matter how detailed the rules, some situations will not be covered. As new problems emerge, additional regulations have to be added. Eventually they become so complicated that people cannot understand them.

God's Laws for Society are not a rule system. Moses referred to "laws and verdicts" (Deut 5:1). God gave a few very basic laws and then added some verdicts as examples of how these laws should be applied in practical situations. These verdicts are not comprehensive, but are sufficient to explain how God's laws should be interpreted and applied.

9. Not too Hard

Living in harmony by complying with God's law is practical, and not beyond the ability of people without the cross and the gospel.

> Now what I am commanding you today is not too difficult
> for you or beyond your reach (Deut 30:11).

God's two laws are not to too difficult for ordinary people. Most people can avoid stealing or assaulting other people. Sin might burst out from time to time and destroy peace, but by dealing with theft and violence, law restrains the worst effects of sin.

10. Sufficient for Peace

Political theorists claim that government is needed to keep order and maintain peace. They believe that without government, crime and violence would destroy society. This view is now widely accepted as a justification for political power.

The Bible teaches something different. Humans will sometimes have violence or thieving in their hearts, but good laws can restrain them. A strong authoritarian political leader is not needed to maintain the peace (according to Samuel, a strong leader will destroy the peace). Good law can restrain violence and theft sufficiently to allow people to live in peace most of the time.

> We know that the law is good if one uses it properly. We
> also know that the law is made not for the righteous but
> for lawbreakers and rebels (1 Tim 1:8-9).

When the law is used for restraining rebels and evildoers, it can produce peace.

11. Spiritual Powers of Evil

The Laws for Society recognise that the spiritual powers of evil often take advantage of situations to cause a person to be harmed by mistake.

> However, if he does not do it intentionally, but the gods
> (spiritual powers of evil) let it happen... (Ex 21:13).

Many accidental injuries are the work of the spiritual powers of evil (Deut 19:5). These should not be treated as crimes.

12. Gracious Gift

God's law was a gracious gift to a world that had rejected him, because it provided relief from sin and evil before the gospel had come. The two most damaging consequences of sin are theft and violence. These have pervaded the entire world, causing terrible suffering and poverty.

- When stealing and theft are normal, poverty follows. If any surplus production is likely to be stolen, being productive is pointless.
- Violence casts a terrible shadow over human life. If violence is everywhere, human life is impossible. If leaving home is dangerous, human interaction is almost impossible. Countering violence often leads to greater violence. Local violence often escalates into war and destruction.

Freedom from theft and violence enables people to concentrate on productive economic activity. They can build labour-saving equipment without fear of it being stolen or destroyed.

Giving his two laws was God's first step towards cleaning up the mess of sin and evil. Any community could make acceptance of the laws against theft and violence a condition for joining. This was not a total solution, because it could not deal with sickness, demons, foolishness and broken relationships, but the law could deal with theft and violence, two of the most harmful consequence of sin.

Rare Use

Law will not be important in the Government of God. If most of the people living in a Kingdom Community are followers of Jesus, law will not be needed much, because theft and violence will be rare. Christians will choose to suffer injustice for love, rather than call on the law.

God's people should only use judges as a last resort after all other possibilities for reconciliation are exhausted. Paul says that lawsuits are a failure of love.

> The very fact that you have lawsuits among you means you
> have been completely defeated already. Why not rather be
> wronged? Why not rather be cheated (1 Cor 6:7).

If someone strikes a Christian, they should not strike back.

> If someone slaps you on one cheek, turn to them the other
> also (Luke 6:29).

If a person steals from a follower of Jesus, their first response will be to bless them.

> Give to everyone who asks you, and if anyone takes what
> belongs to you, do not demand it back (Luke 6:30).

If the Holy Spirit is moving and releasing the fruit of the Spirit, love should be flowing in the community. If most people are following Jesus, they will usually live in peace, so theft and violence will be uncommon. Even when they do occur, followers of Jesus will prefer love-based solutions to law-based solutions.

As more and more people choose to follow Jesus, the role of law should diminish. If most of society is following him, the law will be nearly redundant. However, kingdom society will never be perfect. Problems that cannot be solved by love will be sorted out by local judges using God's law.

Some residents of a community will have chosen not to follow Jesus. They will need law and judges to deal with any theft or violence that affects them. Christians will not use judges much, but they will provide wise judges to apply God's law on behalf of the people they live amongst.

If the gospel fades and love grows cold within a Kingdom Community, more people will need the law and judges. From time to time, the love of the Holy Spirit will be lost and faith will fall away. When people reject the grace of the gospel and forget how to love, God's two laws can restrain the worst effects of sin. When a Christian society degenerates, the law will be a backstop that holds it together despite the advance of sin.

Two Standards

A Kingdom Community will have two different standards.

1. Citizens of the Kingdom will be expected to live by the gospel standards, because they have received the Spirit. Their law is Jesus' new commandment.

> Love one another, as I have loved you.
> Turn the other cheek
> Give to those who ask for help.

   This type of behaviour should be normal for Christians, but it will not be expected from those who have not chosen to follow Jesus.

2. Residents within a Kingdom Community who have not chosen to follow Jesus will be expected to live according to God's Laws for Society.

No stealing or theft.

No assault or murder.

If they want the benefits of living among a Kingdom Community, they will have to accept God's law. (The same law will apply to citizens who have fallen away from their faith.) They will often benefit from Christian love, but they will not be expected to live by Christian standards.

The leaders of the community will say to the people living among them something like this.

> We do not expect you to live according to the standards of Jesus, but you will recognise the need for good law. We are offering you the best set of laws possible. We will apply them, if you are willing to accept them. That is all that you need to do to have a part in this community.

That is an offer that would be hard to refuse, as this standard will not be too hard for most people.

Christian Reluctance

Although God has given good Laws for Society, Christians have been reluctant to accept them. It is not surprising that the world hates God's law, but it is odd that his own people are equally hostile. Several reasons are given for preferring human laws to God's law, but none is valid.

Some Christians assume that God's law was only for ancient Israel. This is not correct, because God expected the nations around Israel to see the wisdom of Israel's law and copy it for themselves (Deut 4:6-8).

Many Christians assume that God's law has been replaced by grace. This is misleading, because Jesus stated clearly that he had not come to abolish the law (Matt 5:17-19). Grace is wonderful, but it does not remove society's need for good laws.

The Law of Moses has often been rejected because Christians assume it is a system of salvation by good works. They believe that God expected the children of Israel to earn his favour by keeping a tough set of rules. This understanding is wrong. The covenant did not require people to be perfect. It did not even try to define holiness. Sins that displease God, such as pride, jealousy, anger, hatred and selfishness are not mentioned in the books of Moses.

God knew the people would keep on sinning, so he provided a system of sacrifices that would deliver forgiveness for sin. These sacrifices could not fully deal with sin, but they pointed forward to the perfect sacrifice of Jesus. The Israelites were relying on what Jesus would do much later, without realising it.

The Pharisees twisted God's good law into a set of rules for proving their righteousness. Jesus rebuked them, saying that they had distorted God's law by transforming it into the traditions of man. They placed an unbearable burden on the people.

> They tie up heavy, cumbersome loads and put them on other people's shoulders, but they themselves are not willing to lift a finger to move them (Matt 23:4).

God never uses law in this way, because he knows that people cannot become righteous by complying with a set of rules.

Even perfect laws cannot make people perfect. Law cannot change human nature. Only the cross and the gospel have that power. God gave the law to restrain the worst sins of theft and violence. That was all that could be done before the cross, all and that he intended.

7

Laws for Society

Big Box

The first five books of the Old Testament are called the Torah. This Hebrew word is often translated as law, but a better translation would be "instruction" or "teaching". The Torah contains God's instruction to the children of Israel about the way they should live. A common Old Testament expression is "dabar torah", which means "Words of the Instruction" (Deut 31:12,24).

The five books of the Torah cover a variety of topics, including:

- creation
- history
- civil laws
- sacrifices
- tabernacle design
- covenants
- infection control and hygiene
- genealogies
- blessings and curses
- rules for priesthood
- land distribution

The Torah is a big box. A lot of different stuff is all mixed up together and sometimes repeated. We need a way to separate God's laws for society from the stuff in the books of Moses that is no longer relevant.

Ten Commandments

When Christians speak of God's law for society, they usually think of the Ten Commandments, but this is not much help. The Ten Commandments get frequent mention, but they are mostly ignored in practice. Most people who claim to live by the Ten Commandments would be hard-pushed to list all ten.

The Ten Commandments were not a set of laws, but a summary of the covenant agreed between God and the children of Israel. Although English translations of the Old Testament refer to the Ten Commandments, a more literal translation is "Ten Words" (Deut 4:13). They are God's most important guidance to Israel about how they should live.

Christians do not live under this covenant with Israel, so we have to assess each of the Ten Words to determine if they are relevant to the Kingdom of God.

- The first three words specify loyalty to God. He reserves the right to judge these three words himself, so they are not laws that human judges can enforce.
    > You shall have no other gods before me.
    > You shall not make for yourself an idol.
    > You shall not misuse the name of the Lord.
  The requirements of these commandments still apply to followers of Jesus. They must honour Jesus as Lord and put no other god before him. The warning about the dangers of idols and images is important in a culture where image is everything, but these sins are not crimes punishable by judges. God can protect his own name.

- The Sabbath was an important cultural marker that distinguished Israel from the surrounding nations. However, Jesus gave us our true rest, and the presence of the Holy Spirit became our defining cultural marker (Heb

4:1-11). Having a weekly rest is good for physical and mental health, but should not be enforced by judges.

- Christians are still expected to honour their parents, but this should now be voluntary, as the Holy Spirit changes hearts and attitudes. Judges are not required to enforce this word.

- The tenth word prohibits coveting, but there is no punishment specified (Ex 20:17). Judges cannot see into another person's heart, so they cannot deal with coveting, unless the coveter acts on their thoughts and translates them into theft.

- The seventh word prohibits adultery, but it was never enforced, even by Moses.

> Jesus replied, "Moses permitted you to divorce your wives because your hearts were hard. But it was not this way from the beginning" (Matt 19:8).

Moses did not enforce the law against adultery, because the people's hearts were hard. There were so many people committing adultery that applying biblical sanctions would have been unacceptable.

God does not want his standards imposed on a society that is opposed to him, as this undermines respect for his law. He has not changed his mind; rather he is realistic about what can be achieved by laws.

- The ninth word is relevant to the judging process (Ex 20:16). Honesty is essential for the working of a judicial system. Witnesses must not give false testimony.

The remaining two of the ten words forbid theft and violence. These are the only two words that God expects judges to apply. This is not controversial because theft and murder are recognised as wrong by everyone everywhere.

Leviticus

The book of Leviticus was specifically directed to the children of Israel and not applicable in other situations. The book begins with God directing Moses to speak to them.

> The Lord called to Moses and spoke to him from the Tent of Meeting. He said, "Speak to the children of Israel" (Lev 1:1-2).

The phrase "Speak to the children of Israel" is used in over half of the chapters of the book (1:2, 4:1, 7:28, 11:1, 12:1, 15:2, 18:1, 20:1, 23:2, 25:1, 27:1). The final verse confirms the book's purpose.

> These are the commands the Lord gave Moses on Mount
> Sinai for the Israelites (Lev 27:34).

The instructions given in this book shape the relationship between God and Israel. They are not universal, but were given for the season before the cross, when the children of Israel had no spiritual protection. They had to ruthlessly separate themselves from the neighbouring peoples, because that was the only way to keep themselves safe from the spiritual forces of evil at work in the surrounding cultures. Leviticus is a "How-To" for the protection of God's people from the spiritual powers of evil prior to the cross.

The cross of Jesus provides much better spiritual protection, so we no longer need to separate ourselves from other cultures. In fact, Jesus told us to go into the world, knowing we will be safe, because the Holy Spirit is with us.

How-To's

A common Hebrew phrase in the book of Leviticus is "Zoth Torah". It is usually translated as "This is the law of" or "This is the regulations for"... (Lev 7:1). A better translation would be "How-To". Leviticus 7:1-10 is the "How-To" for the guilt offering. The book of Leviticus includes a large number of How-To's. There is one for each of the offerings. There is also a How-To for the consecration of priests, for holy food, for childbirth, for skin diseases and religious festivals. (The phrase Zoth Torah is also used in the book of Numbers). The How-To's are not laws, but instruction manuals for the Israelites when they entered the land. They are not universal commands for everyone.

Jesus

Jesus came to fulfil the law (Mat 5:17). That means that some parts of the law are obsolete, because they were fulfilled by his death and resurrection. The temple, priesthood and tabernacle sacrifices are no longer needed, because they were fulfilled by Jesus' perfect sacrifice on the cross.

Laws for Everyone

Detecting laws that are no long applicable is straightforward, but picking those that are universally applicable in every culture in every age is more difficult. We need a way to identify God's universal laws for society.

The key to identifying the universal laws for society is a phrase in the book of Exodus. Whereas most laws in Exodus are addressed to Israel, a section in the middle of Exodus is addressed to a "universal man". Each command begins with the expression, "If a man" (kiy ish). This marks them out as laws for all people. This set of universal laws begins at Exodus 21:12 and ends at Exodus 22:17.

This section stands out as being different, because it is expressed in the third person. Most of the other laws in Exodus are expressed in the second person: you shall not steal, you shall not murder. Moses used the pronoun "you", because he was addressing Israel and announcing laws for his listeners and their descendants.

The laws beginning at Exodus 21:12 have the form: "if he does something, he shall receive this penalty". This mode of speech is used when referring to someone who is not part of the conversation. It points to a third person (he), who is not the speaker (me) and not the listener (you). Moses used the third person here, because this section of laws are for all people and not just for those who participate in the covenant made on Mount Sinai. In Exodus 22:18-19 Moses switched back to the second person and stopped using the expression "if a man", indicating that he had reverted to speaking to Israel.

The subject of the verb is always "a man" or "men". There is no definite article, so the reference is not to a particular man, but to any man. These are laws for all men and women.

Exodus 21:12 to Exodus 22:17 sets out Laws for Society that can be applied to all societies everywhere. God gave these laws to protect people from evil and provide justice within their community. The penalties for failure to comply are specified in a timeless way so they can be applied by judges in any culture.

Law for Society
The Laws for Society given to Moses cover two areas of life:
- protection of property
- personal injury.

1. Protection of Property
Exodus 22:1-16 deals with protection of property. These laws define the nature of theft and specify appropriate remedies.

If a man steals an ox or a sheep… (v.1).

If a man causes a field or vineyard to be grazed over, or lets his beast loose and it feeds in another man's field… (v.5).

If a man gives to his neighbour money or goods to keep safe, and it is stolen from the man's house… (v.7)

If a man gives to his neighbour a donkey or an ox or a sheep or any beast to keep safe, and it dies or is injured… (v.10).

If a man borrows anything from his neighbour, and it is injured or dies, the owner not being with it… (v.14).

The laws apply to any person who undertakes the action specified. They are not limited to the children of Israel.

The seduction of a young woman is also a form of theft.

If a man seduces a virgin, and lies with her (22:16).

He has stolen the most precious thing that she has. Loss of virginity might prevent her from finding a good husband. The man who has robbed her of this potential must compensate here financially for what she has lost, including emotional harm.

2. Personal Injury
The second half of Exodus 21 deals with protection from personal injury. The modern terms are assault and murder. Murder is the most serious form of assault. These laws are expressed in the same way as those that deal with theft.

If a man willfully attacks another to kill him by cunning… (v.14).

If men quarrel and one strikes the other with a stone or with his fist… (v.18).

If a man hits his manservant or maidservant with a rod… (v.21).

If men who are fighting hit a pregnant woman and she gives birth prematurely… (v.22).

If a man hits a manservant or maidservant in the eye and destroys it… (v.26).

If a bull gores a man or a woman to death… (v.28).

If a man opens a pit, or digs a pit and does not cover it… (v.33)

If a man's ox butts another's… (v.35).

These laws define the scope of assault and are universal in application. They are not directed to a particular people, but to all people everywhere.

Murder is a assault with fatal consequences. It is an unlawful assault that kills another person.

Nothing Else

God's Laws for Society have just two objectives.

- Protection of property
- Protection of human life

God has specified only two types of sin for which a remedy or punishment can be imposed by a human court. In his system of justice, judges are limited to dealing with two types of behaviour.

- Theft or damage to property
- Physical injury to a human person.

These two offences are the only ones specified in the Laws for Society. There is nothing else. This makes God's law simple and easy for everyone to understand. It means that we do not need hordes of legislators producing thousands of pages of new legislation each year. All we need is wise judges, who can decide in any situation, whether a victim was assaulted, or if their property was or stolen.

The simplicity of these laws demonstrates the brilliant wisdom of God. In twenty-five verses, he gives a set of laws that will function in any culture at any time. Moses gives sufficient sample verdicts to allow judges to decide when a crime has occurred. This means that they are just as applicable in a modern industrialised culture as in a simple agrarian culture. Judges can decide the appropriate restitution that should be made to compensate for the crime in any culture or type of economy.

Human lawmakers have worked for hundreds of years and produced thousands of statutes, but they have not been able to produce a system of laws for society that works as well. What human lawmakers have failed to do, God did three thousand years ago using just a thousand words.

Laws for Residents

Followers of Jesus must not use government power to impose Jesus' standards on the world. The Laws of Society are his standard for people without the Holy Spirit. The requirements are minimal.

- Do not steal.
- Do not assault people.

This is all that God requires of the people of the world. He would prefer that they did not commit adultery, because it destroys the structure of families and society, but that is asking too much for people without the Spirit working in their lives. God does not expect residents within Kingdom Communities to live according Jesus' commands. He provided an easier standard for people who have not chosen to follow Jesus in the Laws for Society.

Interpreting the Law

The longest Psalm urges those who seek wisdom and justice to love God's law.

> Oh, how I love your law!
> I meditate on it all day long.
> Your commands make me wiser than my enemies,
> for they are ever with me.
> I have more insight than all my teachers,
> for I meditate on your statutes.
> I have more understanding than the elders,
> for I obey your precepts.
> Righteous are you, O Lord,
> and your laws are right.
> The statutes you have laid down are righteous;
> they are fully trustworthy (Psalm 119:97-100,137-138).

Laws for Society

Loving the law inspires a different approach to its interpretation. My method for interpreting the law in this book is based on the following principles.

- The scriptures were breathed by the Holy Spirit (2 Tim 3 16). We do not know how involved Moses was in the process of recording the law, but that does not matter, because the Holy Spirit was at work. He got the stuff that he wanted into the books of Moses. This means that the best way to understand the Laws for Society is to look for what the Holy Spirit is saying.

- The Laws for Society must be interpreted through the lens of Jesus' life and teaching. His life was the full and final revelation of God's character, so the gospels are essential for understanding the meaning of God's laws. Moses often misunderstood what he received from God, but Jesus' understanding of the law was perfect. Jesus condemned bad interpretations, but he never repudiated the Laws for Society, so they must contain a message that is consistent with his gospel.

- Jesus explained to the disciples he met on the road to Emmaus that Moses and the prophets had written about him (Luke 24:27). Our interpretations of the law must reveal Jesus.

- The law and the gospels were inspired by the Holy Spirit, so they will be consistent with each other. If the laws of Moses seem to be inconsistent with the New Testament, then we have misunderstood them, or the translators have mistranslated them.

- We must not use the behaviour of the Israelites to interpret the Laws for society. Their behaviour often fell short of God's standard, so it can never be normative.

- Archaeological information from the surrounding nations is not very useful for interpreting the Laws for society, as they were controlled by evil spiritual principalities and powers that hate God. The practices of the Babylonians cannot provide insights into the meaning of God's law.

- Hebrew is not a precise language like Greek. The words are sparse, so they can take many meanings. Hebrew is a very old language, so the meaning of many Hebrew words is uncertain. We should always choose the meaning that is consistent with the New Testament.
- We cannot rely on the interpretations and translations of Jewish scholars, because they have a tendency to cast a violent shadow over the law to justify Israel's history of violence and war. They tend to choose the harshest possible meaning of a passage, whereas we need one that is consistent with the gospel. We have a huge advantage over them, because we can read the Laws of Society with the guidance of the Holy Spirit.
- Most Christian translators and interpreters of the Old Testament want to emphasise the difference between law and grace. They have been content to make the Old Testament seem harsh and cruel, because it makes the gospel look better. They do not understand that the Laws of Society are a gift of grace, but with a different purpose.

In this book, I will often seem to push the boundary of the meaning of some well-known passages. That is deliberate, because I am translating and interpreting them in a way that is consistent with the Gospel. I believe that is the best way to understand what the Holy Spirit is saying.

Jesus and the Laws of Society
When announcing the gospel of the Kingdom, Jesus often pointed back to the Laws of Society.

- Jesus promised blessings for those who are merciful.
  > Blessed are the merciful, for they will be shown
  > mercy (Matt 5:7).

  The Law promises blessings so it must be merciful. If we think it is not merciful, we have not understood it.
- In the Sermon on the Mount, Jesus distinguished between the laws given to Moses and more recent local sayings.
  > You have heard that it was said, 'Love your
  > neighbour and hate your enemy.' But I tell you,

love your enemies (Matt 5:43-44).

Much of what they had heard about the law was not in it. The law did not command them to hate their enemies. Jesus taught them what the law really said. Unfortunately, many Christians interpret the law as if it requires us to hate our enemies.

Jesus claimed that the Jewish establishment had misunderstood the law. They turned it into something harsh and cruel. If it is applied correctly, it will bring blessing to the poor and mercy for the weak. Those who think the law is harsh and cruel are wrong.

- Jesus warned that the Teachers of the Law did not understand it.

     Their teachings are merely human rules (Mark 7:7).

He wants a different understanding of the law. The traditions of men are an obstacle to the Kingdom of God.

> You have let go of the commands of God and are holding on to traditions of men (Mark 7:8).

> Woe to you, teachers of the law and Pharisees, you hypocrites! You shut the door of the kingdom of heaven in people's faces. You yourselves do not enter, nor will you let those enter who are trying to (Matt 23:13).

> Woe to you experts in the law, because you have taken away the key to knowledge. You yourselves have not entered, and you have hindered those who were entering (Luke 11:52).

The teachers of the law and the Pharisees got the law wrong and closed off its insights into the Kingdom of God. We must not make the same mistake. The Government of God needs a totally different approach to the Law.

- Jesus interpreted the Law in a way that made life better for people. His approach was very different from the miserable and mean interpretation of the Teachers of the Law.

> Woe to you also, lawyers! For you load men with burdens hard to bear, and you yourselves do not touch the burdens with one of your fingers (Luke 11:46).

81

Interpretations of the law that place an impossible burden on people are wrong.

- Jesus claimed that loving our neighbour is nearly as important as loving God.

> The second is like it: 'Love your neighbour as yourself (Matt 22:39).

Love of neighbour is the heart of the Law. Therefore, we must read the law through the lens of love for our neighbours, remembering that everyone in our community is a neighbour.

The parable of the Good Samaritan was a message about the law. The Priest and the Levite complied with a traditional interpretation of the law, but they did not understand it. Jesus exposed their problem, but we continue to accept a Jewish interpretation of the law. People seeking the Kingdom of God must apply the law in the same way as the Good Samaritan.

The Law of Moses is the most important scripture, apart from the gospels, because it was given directly by God on the mountain. It should come ahead of Paul's letters and the prophets in our thinking about the organisation of society. However, we must apply it in the way that Jesus interpreted it.

Law of Love

Law and love are not opposites. Paul says that fulfilling the law and living by love are the same. This is an amazing statement.

> Love does no harm to its neighbour. Therefore love is the fulfilment of the law (Rom 13:10).

The law is not the opposite of love, but is consistent with it. Love does no harm to another person, so good law cannot allow harm to anyone. A system of justice that forces people to do things against their will would be inconsistent with love.

God's law is the only law that can be fulfilled by love. Love could never fulfil modern systems of law, because they are far too complicated. Modern systems of law are deficient, because they cannot be fulfilled by love.

8
Local Judges

Law and judges are essential for justice.

- Justice needs law, because people need to know before they act, whether an action is lawful.
- Justice needs judges to decide if the law has been broken and what should be the remedy.

God revealed his Laws for Society to Moses. We need good judges to apply his good laws.

Excellent Judges

In God's system of justice, judges emerge as people recognise wise elders within their local communities and go to them for guidance about their disputes. When the wisdom of an elder is recognised widely, people will start referring to them as a judge. The title is recognition of what they are already doing.

The community validates more excellent judges by observing the wisdom of their decisions and taking their cases to them. This is why the scriptures urge us to submit to excellent judges.

> Every person should submit to the more excellent judges, because the judges that are are put in place by God (Rom 13:1).

Excellent judges are not appointed to their role, but are recognised when people submit their cases to them. As more and more people submit their cases to good decision-makers, they will be recognised as excellent judges.

By submitting to excellent judges, we allow God to raise up the judges that he has chosen. Only judges that come into their positions through voluntary submission have legitimate authority (more on Romans 13 in chapter 9).

Excellent judges can only emerge, if people are free to choose a judge to decide their case. If they have this freedom, they will choose those whose wisdom and skill are recognised by people that they trust. The process will work best if people know potential judges personally, or trust people who know them.

Moses Released Judges

While the Israelites were slaves in Egypt, their taskmasters settled all disputes, so they did not need judges. When they escaped Egypt, they had no judges and did not understand the process by which judges could emerge in society.

Moses assumed that he should be the sole judge and tried to hear every case, but God had not given him this role. He was a prophet. God delivered the law through him, because his calling made him skilled at hearing the voice of God. Part of this prophetic role was teaching the law to the people, but God did not appoint him to be the judge of the nation.

Moses assumed that God wanted him to be chief judge, so he exhausted himself by trying to hear every dispute. Jethro challenged Moses, so he allowed the people to take their disputes to the wisest people in their families, clans and tribes.

> They served as judges for the people at all times. The difficult cases they brought to Moses, but the simple ones they decided themselves (Ex 18:26).

Moses released people whose wisdom was already trusted in their families and communities to become judges.

Becoming a Judge

The wisdom of potential judges will be recognised by their families. When they resolve disputes between members of their family, others will notice their wisdom and take their disagreements to them. If a wise person is successful in settling disputes in their wider family, they will begin to recognised in their community for their skill in judging. People will refer their disputes to them to get the benefit of their wisdom.

Excellent judges will be identified by a natural sifting process. Many people will demonstrate wisdom in their families, but only a few will have sufficient wisdom to deal with the more complicated interactions of the local community. The few who gain a reputation across the wider community for wise decisions will be recognised as judges.

The members of the community can influence the reputation of a judge, by accepting their decisions. If people undermine the decisions of a judge, people with disputes will avoid them.

No Monopoly

The Law of Moses always speaks about judges in the plural (Ex 22:8-9; Deut 19:17-18; 25:1). People will get better justice when a number of judges are competing to provide a better service. The influence of good judges will expand when people are free to choose between judges.

In the modern world, the civil government controls the judicial process. Litigants have to use the judges employed by the government. Unfortunately, monopoly power tends to increase the price and reduce the quality of a service. The cost of maintaining the judicial system has increased dramatically, while obtaining justice takes longer and longer.

Judges must not be appointed by political leaders, because the person with the power of appointment has the ability to distort justice. Judges appointed by kings or politicians lose their freedom, because those who appoint them can also remove them.

Each community should have several judges whom people can choose between. If people are free to choose a judge to hear their case, no judge will have a monopoly over judging.

Some judges might specialise in particular types of case. A local judge might never get to deal with a complicated insurance case. Judges who understand a particular aspect of law might begin to specialise in particular types of cases.

Disagreements about Judges

The parties to a legal dispute will have to agree on their judge. This may be problematic if one person wants one judge, but the other wants a different one. The best way might be to choose a judge from a neighbouring community, who is less connected to the litigants. Another solution would be for both parties to choose their preferred judge, and for these two judges to choose a third judge to sit on the case with them to balance their views. Agreement on an independent judge would ensure justice is fair.

The victim of a crime will have priority in choosing a judge to hear their case. A criminal will not be able to avoid justice, by refusing to agree to a judge. If they refuse to agree, the judge chosen by the victim should proceed to hear the case. If the judge has a reputation for fairness, the people will back their verdict.

Free Authority

Local judges exercise Free Authority, because they gain authority when the people submit their disputes to them. If people stop bringing cases, the judge loses authority and their role is done.

- The authority of judges is limited, because their authority is confined to the situation submitted to them. They have no authority over other aspects of their litigant's lives.
- A judge's authority is temporary. When a case has been decided and the required restitution paid, the authority delegated to the judge disappears. Even during a trial, the parties to the dispute can withdraw their submission, if they think the judge is unfair. They have freely submitted to the judge, so they can withdraw their submission at any time.
- The authority of judges is fragile, because they never gain permanent authority. The most they can get is a reputation for wisdom, but a reputation is never permanent and a serious mistake can destroy it. A judge with a good reputation will be given authority to hear cases in the future, but a judge who makes bad decisions will lose their reputation and people will stop submitting cases to them.

A judge's authority is not permanent. It is limited, temporary and fragile.

Christian Judges

A Kingdom Community will be an environment where good judges can emerge and be recognised. Most will begin as an elder in a neighbourhood church. An elder with a prophetic edge might be recognised for their wisdom.

Paul reminded Christians that there should always be people among them who can resolve difficult disputes. One problem with the Corinthian church was that wise judges were not emerging as Paul expected.

> If any of you has a dispute with another, do you dare to take it before the ungodly for judgment instead of before the Lord's people?... Therefore, if you have disputes about such matters, do you ask for a ruling from those whose way of life is scorned in the church? I say this to shame you. Is it possible that there is nobody among you wise enough to judge a dispute between believers (1 Cor 6:1, 4-5)?

Christians should take their disagreements to their elders. Most neighbourhood churches will have a least one who is capable of making wise decisions.

Some elders will develop a reputation in their church for handling disputes wisely. As their reputation spreads, other residents of the Kingdom Community will submit their disputes to these wise elders (1 Tim 3:7).

Solomon received "the wisdom of God to administer justice" (1 Kings 3:28). We should expect that God would raise up elders with similar wisdom. Now that the Holy Spirit has been poured out, the wisdom of Solomon should be common amongst the followers of Jesus.

Elders with the "wisdom of God to administer justice" will be respected in their community and sought out by the people of the world needing justice.

> Do you not know that the saints will judge the world (1 Cor 6:2)?

This is not a reference to the "last judgment". The people of the world will recognise the ability of wise elders and be drawn to them in the same way that pagan kings from all over the world came to listen to Solomon.

The whole world sought audience with Solomon to hear
the wisdom God had put in his heart (1 Kings 10:24).
Everyone will come to the elders of a Kingdom Community to
receive the wisdom that God has put in their hearts.

Character of Judges

Good judges will be impartial and honest. Moses challenged
judges with the following words.

Judge fairly, whether the case is between brother Israelites or
between one of them and an alien. Do not show partiality in
judging; hear both small and great alike. Do not be afraid of
any man, for judgment belongs to God. Bring me any case too
hard for you, and I will hear it (Deut 1:16-17).

Good judges will decide on the merits of the case, ignoring the
status of those making claims. Foreigners and refugees should be
able to obtain judgment without any bias against them.

Judges must not favour people who are rich or important. Nor
should they favour the poor.

Do not pervert justice; do not show partiality to the poor
or favouritism to the great, but judge your neighbour fairly
(Lev 19:15).

The judges must pursue the truth without fear or favour to
anyone. Rich and poor must be treated the same.

Judges must not accept bribes.

Do not pervert justice or show partiality. Do not accept a
bribe, for a bribe blinds the eyes of the wise and twists the
words of the righteous. Follow justice and justice alone, so
that you may live and possess the land the Lord your God
is giving you (Deut 16:19-20).

Judge carefully, for with the Lord our God there is no
injustice or partiality or bribery (2 Chron 19:7).

Good judges must remember that they are acting on behalf of
God. They should fear the Lord and judge carefully.

Judges that depend on people in their community submitting
disputes to them will have a strong incentive to be fair to
everyone. If they lose their reputation for fairness, they will soon
be out of a job.

Local Judges

Good judges will be anointed by the Holy Spirit. Jesus was the perfect judge, because he was full of the Holy Spirit and carried a Spirit of wisdom and counsel.

> The Spirit of the Lord will rest on him—
> the Spirit of wisdom and of understanding,
> the Spirit of counsel and of power (Isaiah 11:2).

Excellent judges will be full of the Holy Spirit and his wisdom. Good judges will know and love God's Laws for Society.

> I hate and abhor falsehood, but I love your law. Seven times a day I praise you for your righteous laws. Great peace have they who love your law, and nothing can make them stumble (Psalm 119:163-165).

Love of God's law will prevent many mistakes.

Bad Judges

Corrupt judges produce injustice by ignoring evidence and deciding in favour of those with money and power. Zephaniah describes some judges as wolves.

> Her judges are evening wolves who leave nothing for the morning (Zeph 3:3).

In many countries, judges look after their mates among the rich and strong. The poor and weak cannot get justice.

> Speak the truth to each other,
> and render true and sound judgment in your courts,
> do not plot evil against your neighbour,
> and do not love to swear falsely.
> "I hate all this," declares the Lord (Zech 8:16-17).

When judges are dishonest or corrupt, the weak will suffer.

Judges appointed by kings or political leaders are dangerous, because they tend to be loyal to those who appointed them. They will have difficulty deciding against their political or religious leaders in favour of ordinary people.

Prophets will have a role in keeping the judges honest. Micah challenged the judges of Jerusalem for accepting bribes.

> Her leaders judge for a bribe, her priests teach for a price,
> and her prophets tell fortunes for money (Mic 3:11).

Prophets will expose bad judges and encourage people to seek excellent ones.

Judges Job

Judges are expected to resolve the cases that are brought before them. There are five aspects to their work.

1. A judge should thoroughly investigate the case by collecting all relevant information (Deut 21:2).

   > The judges must make a thorough investigation (Deut 19:18).

2. The judge should listen to all the relevant witnesses.

   > A matter must be established by the testimony of two or three witnesses (Deut 19:15).

3. The judge must arrive at a verdict (Ex 18:22).

   > The judges will decide the case, acquitting the innocent and condemning the guilty (Deut 25:1).

   The verdict will acquit those who are innocent and condemn those who are guilty.

4. The judge must announce the truth.

   > They will declare to you the verdict in the case (Deut 17:9).

   The judge declares the truth about the claims of the victim. If the judge accepts the victim's case, they are vindicated. One meaning of "tsedeq", the Hebrew word for justice is vindication. When justice is done, the victims of the injustice are vindicated.

   The other side of the verdict is a declaration about the actions of the person accused. If the claims of the accuser are upheld, the person accused is declared guilty. If the accusation is incorrect, the accused person is vindicated.

5. A judge must specify the remedy required by the law.

   > Act according to their word of direction (Deut 17:10).

   The verdict of the judge includes actions to put right the injustice. The judge will determine what remedy is prescribed by God's Laws for Society. This action should restore the victim to what their situation would have been if the injustice had not occurred. Reconciliation between the two parties to the dispute is the ultimate goal.

A judge's voice is prophetic. Their verdict is a judgment on the guilty person. If they do not agree to the required restitution, the declaration of guilt leaves them vulnerable to attack by the spiritual powers of evil. The verdict also releases the blessing of the Holy Spirit onto the person who is vindicated.

Multiple Witnesses

A key principle in God's Laws for Society is that a person can only be convicted of a crime on the evidence of at least two independent witnesses. Hearsay is not sufficient.

> One witness is not enough to convict a man accused of any crime or offence he may have committed. A matter must be established by the testimony of two or three witnesses (Deut 19:15).

The requirement for two or three witnesses imposes a high standard for convicting a person of a crime. It prevents a person from making false charges against someone they do not like. Another person must confirm their evidence. For serious crimes, there must be at least three witnesses.

The witnesses must be independent and unbiased. They must not have committed the crime which they are testifying about John 8:7). For example, people with a record for violence cannot be witnesses to crimes of violence.

One reason for multiple witnesses is to ensure that innocent people are not convicted. The price of this caution is that criminals will sometimes "get away" with their crimes. This is not a problem, as their escape from justice is only temporary. They will not escape the perfect judge at the final judgement.

> For we must all appear before the judgement seat of Christ, so that each one may receive what is due for what he has done in the body, whether good or evil (2 Cor 5:10).

Justice is certain. Those escaping the punishment of judges in this age will receive perfect justice when they stand before God.

Appeals

God has perfect knowledge, so only his judgments are always true.

> Salvation and glory and power belong to our God,
> for true and just are his judgments (Rev 19:1-2).

Human judges aim for the truth, but their judgements will sometimes fall short. The best protection against judges missing the truth is a strong appeal process.

All people affected by a decision made by a local judge must be free to appeal the case to another judge, if they think the decision is unfair. An appeal will usually be taken by the loser of a case, but a winner who is confident in their case will be happy to go to appeal so that doubt is eliminated.

An appeal would need reasonable grounds to get consideration by a good judge. If a decision is obviously correct, a wise judge would not want to hear an appeal. Excellent judges will protect their reputation by avoiding frivolous cases. This will prevent people from shopping around to find a judge to give them the decision they want.

Appeals have an educative function. By watching the decisions of more experienced judges, new judges can learn how to decide cases in the future. The appeal process will expose unwise judges. If a judge is constantly having decisions overturned, people will stop going to them and they will cease to be a judge.

Appeal Judges

Once Moses released local judges to their role, he acted as an appeal judge (Ex 18:25-27). He was equipped for this role, because God had given the law through him, so he understood it best. No one was appointed to this role of appeal judge after he died. People wanting justice chose to appeal their case to judges with a reputation for good decisions.

The initial appeal will go to another judge in the same town. The benefit of multiple judges is that another local judge will be able to hear an appeal. For serious issues, an appeal could be made to a judge in a larger town, who might be experienced at dealing with that particular type of case (Deut 17:8).

Some of the wisest judges will specialise in hearing appeals. Several judges might hear an appeal on a tough case together. An appeal judge might invite other widely respected judges to hear the case together with them, so they can share the responsibility. This will improve the quality of the decision and strengthen the sense of justice (Deut 17:8; 25:1). The decisions of appeal judges will never be perfect, but they will be corrected when we stand before the ultimate court of appeal at the end of the age.

Paying Judges

Being a judge will usually be a part-time role. Most local communities will not have enough cases to occupy a full-time judge. Most will earn their living by pursuing another career.

If a case is complicated and involves a lot of work for the judge, litigants might be requested to pay costs. The person bringing the case would have a responsibility to cover the costs of the judges. One reason for fourfold restitution is to provide enough compensation to cover the judge's expenses. The biblical principle that a workman is worthy of his wages would apply (1 Tim 5:18).

Judges hearing many appeals might need payment for their work. The people of a community might pay a wise person a retainer, so that a trusted judge is available to hear cases when they arise. This would give the judge time to study God's law and keep up-to-date with decisions being made by other judges, but all contributions to the retainer must be voluntary.

Everyone living in a community benefits from good justice, so they owe a debt to the judges who provide it. God's people must decide what they owe good judges for maintaining a peaceful society, and settle the debt owed. Being paid a retainer does not give a judge any authority. People would not have to submit their cases to the judge their community supports. They would be free to go to another judge, if they chose.

Judges with a widespread reputation might develop a business acting as an arbitrator for commercial disputes. A voluntary process for resolving disputes between businesses in different regions and nations will be important for trade.

Perfect System

The gifts of the Spirit are the fulfilment of God's promise to restore wise judges to administer his Laws for Society.

> I will restore your judges as in days of old,
> your counsellors as at the beginning.
> Afterward you will be called the City of Righteousness,
> the Faithful City (Is 1:26).

When judges are full of the Holy Spirit, justice flows.

9
Excellent Judges

Christians often justify human political institutions using Romans 13:1 as a slogan. They kill debate about political power with these slogans:

> *God has established all human governments.*
> *We must submit to every governing authority.*

Because these slogans come from Paul's letter to Romans, Christians assume they settle the argument.

This type of slogan has been used to justify almost all forms of human government. The common argument is that Paul was writing to the church in Rome at a time when Nero was Caesar. If a terrible ruler like Nero was instituted by God, then all forms of political power are justified, so Christians must submit to every political authority that comes to power.

Using Nero to justify an interpretation of this passage sounds odd, but commentators claim that God instituted kings and parliaments to maintain order in society. They assume that life would be awful without human government, so Nero was part of God's order, even though he was evil.

This is nonsense. Rulers like Hitler and Stalin opposed God and slaughtered millions of innocent people. To describe them as servants of God is absurd. Paul knew better than most that the state can be very hostile to God's purposes. Given his experience, it is absurd to suggest he taught that all political authorities are God's servants. His teaching in Romans 13 is not a blanket approval for all political rulers. Because Paul's words have been misused, I will devote an entire chapter to them.

Twisted Logic

The traditional interpretation of Romans 13:1 says that we must submit to all political authorities, because their authority has been given to them by God. To see the twisted logic of this teaching, look at the following sets of statements.

> All authority is ordained by God
> Hitler has authority
> Hitler is ordained by God, so we must submit to him.

This following example exaggerates the point.

> All authority is ordained by God
> Satan has authority.
> Satan is ordained by God, so we must submit to him.

The correct logic is as follows.

> All legitimate authority is from God.
> Hitler and Satan are hostile to God.
> Therefore, the authority of Hitler and Satan is illegitimate.

The statement that all authority is ordained by God cannot be used to legitimise any and every political authority. It should inspire us to seek out legitimate authority.

Context

Treating Romans 13:1 as a political theory in one verse rips it out of context. Paul actually began this teaching about dealing with evil in the previous chapter. He is quite blunt. Evil cannot beat evil. Evil can only be overcome by good.

> Do not be overcome by evil, but overcome evil with good
> (Rom 12:21).

This is consistent with Jesus' teaching. We cannot overcome evil with evil, but must overcome evil with good.

If this is what Paul believed, he would not go on to say the opposite in the next line of his letter. Yet the traditional interpretation of Romans 13:1 implies that evil can be overcome by evil. It suggests that evil rulers are useful, because they bring order to society by restraining evil. However, this would be overcoming evil with evil, which is the opposite of what Paul has stated emphatically in the previous verse. The prophets condemn those who say that evil things are good.

Woe to those who call evil good and good evil (Is 5:20).

We must be careful not to fall into the same trap. If we say that evil rulers are God's servants to do us good, we are saying that bad government is good. We are claiming to overcome evil with evil. We need an understanding of Romans 13 that does not require us to use evil to overcome evil.

Misleading Translation

The way that Romans 13 has been translated is a serious problem. Whenever a word has alternative meanings, the translators tend to choose the sense that gives the greatest support to state power. This is not surprising. Martin Luther, the first of the Protestants to translate the New Testament, was protected by Prince Frederick. He was hardly going to translate Romans 13 in a way that undermined his protector's political power. The translators of the King James Version were not going to translate Romans 13 in a way that denied the power of King James.

Unfortunately, modern translators of the New Testament have followed the example of their predecessors. They continue to translate the passage in a way that supports state power. This is quite odd. An important theme of Paul's letters is that Jesus is Lord, and Caesar is not, so we should not be translating his letters in a way that maximizes Caesar's power. We need a translation of Romans 13 that respects Jesus as Lord.

Kings and parliaments cannot exercise authority that belongs to God. If they understood God's authority, they would know that their power has no place in his kingdom and would be working for the implementation of his government and the dissolution of their positions. None of them are doing this, so they are operating with illegitimate authority stolen from Jesus.

Paul was warning kings and emperors that they are rebels and usurpers; exactly the opposite of the traditional interpretation. Romans 13 must be translated in a way that is consistent with the authority of God and the victory of Jesus on the cross.

The Powers that Be

The key to understanding Romans 13:1 is the strange expression "the powers that be" that crept from the King James Version into modern language.

> ***The powers that be*** are ordained of God (Rom 13:1b).

The conjunction of the plural "powers" with a singular verb "be" sounds odd. The word "powers" is a translation of the Greek word "exousia". This word is often used for a "judge", so the expression could be translated "as the judges that be". This makes the link to the Old Testament clear. Paul is referring back to important statements about judges in Deuteronomy.

> The two people involved in the dispute must stand in the presence of the Lord before the ***judges that shall be*** in those days (Deut 19:17).

> You shall come to the ***judge that shall be*** in those days: and you shall inquire; and they will tell you the word of judgment (Deut 17:9).

The modern translations refer to the "judges that are in office in those days", but the word "office" does not exist in the Hebrew text. A literal translation would be "the judges that shall be in those days" or the "the judges that are in those days". Paul would have been familiar with these texts. When he started thinking about justice and government, the Holy Spirit brought these words to his mind.

These two verses summarise the system of justice and government that God gave through the Mosaic covenant: God's law applied by godly judges. In Romans 13:1, Paul was referring back to Deuteronomy and confirming that God's system of justice had not changed. He was not providing a justification for state power.

Governing Authorities

A good example of the translation problem is the following.

> Everyone must submit to the governing authorities (huperecho exousiais).

This translation is quite misleading, as the word "governing" is not in the Greek text. The word often translated as "governing" is "huperecho". It can mean "superior in rank", but it also has a strong sense of "excellence". Paul used this word in Phil 3:8, when speaking of the "surpassing greatness" of knowing Christ.

In Romans 13:1, Paul is actually saying that Christians should only submit to judges who are excellent. He is giving people with disputes a choice when submitting to a judge. They should only submit to judges who have demonstrated excellence. Paul was not authorising modern political power, but advocating **excellent judges** applying God's law.

> Every person should submit to the more excellent judges, because the judges that are were put in place by God (Rom 13:1).

The word "exousiais" is plural. Paul is not talking about a single leader. He is suggesting that we should submit to judges (plural). The benefit of having many judges is that people have a choice. They can choose the one that is best.

In most modern countries, the state claims a monopoly on judging. Litigants have to use the judge appointed by the state, regardless of their reputation. The Old Testament always speaks of multiple judges (Ex 22:8-9; Deut 19:17-18; 25:1). People must be free to choose a judge to hear their case. Paul is simply confirming this principle.

Not Appointed

We are required to submit to the judges that God has established.

> The judges that are were put in place by God (Rom 13:1b).

Paul seems to imply that these judges just exist. They are not elected or appointed, they just are. This sounds odd, but it is really important.

If judges are appointed, the person who has the power to appoint them has the power to distort justice. Judges appointed by kings or politicians lose their independence, because those who appoint them can also remove them. The people also lose their freedom to choose the best judges.

The Bible describes a better way. Judges emerge as people take their cases to people who demonstrate wisdom. If a person gets a reputation for making wise decisions, more and more people will submit their cases to them and they will gradually be recognised as a judge. Excellent judges are not appointed, they emerge as people recognise the excellence of their wisdom.

Poorer judges will get less and less cases, as people hear about their mistakes, and take their cases to better ones. By submitting to excellent judges, we allow God to put in place (tassa) the judges he has chosen.

Worldly Rulers

People who reject the perfect system of justice that God has provided will find themselves controlled by a worldly ruler.

> Worldly rulers cause no fear for the good way, but only for those choosing the bad option (Rom 13:3).

Followers of Jesus have a choice between God's "good way" and the "bad option". The bad option is life under a worldly ruler.

The word used for "ruler" is "arkon". They are rulers that are opposed to God and are usually controlled by powerful government-spirits. Choosing to live under a worldly ruler is a bad choice because they produce fear/terror, not peace.

Paul had to be careful when warning about rulers. His letter was being sent to the heart of the empire, so he had to use words that would not put his readers at risk from the Roman authorities. The letter would be carried by a messenger, probably Phoebe (Rom 16:1-2). If the language was too incendiary, Phoebe would be in big trouble if the authorities challenged her mission. People who would hold a copy of the letter had to be protected.

Paul gives a subtle warning to the believers in Rome by putting together the words "ruler" and "fear". The recipients of the letter in Rome knew all about the fear of worldly rulers because they had experienced it. Roman power did not provide peace or justice; it protected the rich and powerful while enslaving the poor and impoverishing the rest of society. Paul never connects the words "ruler" with "peace" or "justice".

God's good option described in Romans 12:1-2 is safer for followers of Jesus because excellent judges applying God's law in their local community reduces the influence of government-spirits in their society. Followers of Jesus living within a community of believers are relatively safe from the fear of evil because they can provide protection and support for each other when evil strikes.

The safest place in a hostile world is the body of Jesus. The functioning of the body is described in Romans 12. Followers of Jesus should be devoted to one another in brotherly love (12:10). They should strengthen and protect the body by sharing in the gifts of the Spirit (12:3-8). They should share with people who are in need and practice hospitality (12:13). People who are supporting each other in the unity and power of the Holy Spirit will be less afraid of a powerful ruler.

In the current season, most followers of Jesus will find themselves living under the government of worldly rulers, even if they do not acknowledge the ruler's authority. Resisting a world ruler is pointless and dangerous. It is better to trust in God and wait for worldly power to collapse under its own weight.

The best way to be free from the terror of a worldly ruler is to do good to all society.

> Now, if you don't want to be afraid of his authority, be doing good, and you will be commended (Rom 13:3).

If the followers of Jesus are supporting each other and caring for the non-believers who live amongst them in their community, it will be hard for political powers to fault them.

Pay What You Owe

Paul explains our responsibility to good judges.

> Give everyone what you owe him (Rom 13:7).

The basic principle is that we should make payment to everyone to whom we owe something. This is relevant for justice, as judges will resolve most cases by deciding that one person should make restitution to the other. However, judges do not have the power to enforce these payments. They rely on the rest of their community putting pressure on the person to pay the restitution. God's people can assist by being a good example. We should pay the restitution specified by judges, even if we think it is unfair.

If the person required to make restitution does not have the money, one of the elders in the community might lend the money to them, so they can settle the case. Repayment of this loan will be voluntary too. Christians can set a good example by repaying these loans quickly. Paul says they should pay the debt quickly.

Political Theory

People looking in Romans 13 for a Christian political theory will be disappointed. Paul was not doing political theology, but re-affirming the system of justice that God had given to Moses when Israel entered the Promised Land and was learning to live together in freedom and peace. God had given an ideal system of justice through Moses, so he did not need to give a new political theory through Jesus or Paul.

In his Sermon on the Mount, Jesus taught his disciples to love their enemies (Matt 5:44). In the middle of his teaching, he confirmed that God's system of justice based on local judges applying his law was not abolished (Matt 5:17-18). He drew on the law for solutions when dealing with social and economic problems. Jesus had very little to say about structures of government, because nothing new was needed.

Paul follows the same pattern. After teaching about responding to evil with love in Romans 12, he endorses the justice system that God gave to Moses by referencing Deuteronomy 17:9 and 19:17 in Romans 13:1. If Christians want a political theory they should stop looking in Romans or the gospels and go back to Deuteronomy.

Clear Message

A better translation of Romans 12:21-13:2 would read like this.

> Do not be overcome by evil, but overcome evil with good. Every person should submit to the more excellent judges because there is no legitimate judicial authority except under God. The judges that have emerged in a free society are arranged by God. Anyone resisting the decision of a good judge (exousia) is rebelling against what God has put in place. Those rejecting it are accepting judgment for themselves. Worldly rulers cause no fear for the good way, but only for those choosing the bad option.

These words should be kept together to give a consistent message.

10

Restoration

To understand the Laws for Society, we must remember the purpose for which they were given. God gave these laws to allow sin-prone people to live together in relative harmony. People often demand more, but that is all that laws can achieve.

The justice provided by local judges will have the following characteristics.

1. **Mercy** – judges should seek to return the law-breaker to a good life.
2. **Restoration** – the victim should be restored to the state they were in before the crime.
3. **Reconciliation** – peace should be restored between the parties to the dispute and within the wider community.
4. **Caution** – innocent people should not be punished.
5. **Deterrence** –the benefits of law breaking should be removed.
6. **Justice** – the remedy should fit the crime.

These elements must be balanced against each other, without any one dominating. However, mercy should triumph over justice (James 2:13), because God is gracious and merciful. His name is,

Yahweh, Yahweh, the compassionate and gracious God,
slow to anger, abounding in love and faithfulness,
maintaining love to thousands, and forgiving wickedness,
rebellion and sin (Ex 34:6-7).

If we think that the Laws for Society require judges to be harsh and vengeful, we have not understood the mercy of God.

Community-based judges who administer justice on God's behalf must show mercy and compassion when dealing with those who have broken the law, particularly those who deserve to die.

> Administer true justice; show mercy and compassion to
> one another (Zech 7:9).

Justice without mercy is not true justice.

Jesus' promise in the Sermon on the Mount is important for judges.

> Blessed are the merciful,
> for they will be shown mercy (Matt 5:7).

Judges who trust in Jesus will realise that they will need mercy when they stand before God. They will be merciful when judging, so they will receive mercy when they are judged on the last day.

> Speak and act as those who are going to be judged by the
> law that gives freedom, because judgment without mercy
> will be shown to anyone who has not been merciful.
> Mercy triumphs over judgment (James 2:12-13).

True justice includes mercy.

Restoration

The Laws for Society are not designed for revenge or punishment of crime. They are designed to restore the peace and unity that was lost when the law was broken. Victims should be restored to the position they were in before the harm was done. The person who has broken the law should also be restored to wholeness, so they stop disturbing society.

In the Laws for Society, the main remedy is financial restitution. The Hebrew word translated as restitution is "shalam". It is used 18 times in the verses about theft of property, although this is sometimes lost in translation. Twice the word is doubled for emphasis. Its basic meaning is "be safe" or "be made complete". By implication, it can mean "reciprocate, make amends, end, finish, full, make good, repay, recompense, requite, make restitution, restore".

The person stealing or damaging the property of another must "make good" the harm done. They must "restore" the situation to the way it was before they committed their crime. The well-known Hebrew word for peace (shalom) comes from "shalam", so it has a strong sense of restoring peace to a situation that has been disrupted.

Theft

The person found guilty of theft must make four or fivefold restitution to the victim of their crime.

> If a man steals an ox or a sheep and slaughters it or sells it,
> he must pay back five head of cattle for the ox and four
> sheep for the sheep (Ex 22:1).

The thief must pay his victim four times the value of what he has stolen. The compensation beyond the value of what was stolen makes up for the cost of tracking down the thief, preparing evidence for the court and covering the costs of the judge.

Fourfold restitution also acts as a deterrent. Thieves will not always be caught, so if they only have to pay back what was stolen, they might decide to take the risk. The fourfold repayment reduces the economic benefits of theft.

Zacchaeus put this principle into practice after Jesus had dined with him. He promised fourfold repayment to anyone he had cheated. Jesus applauded his actions, confirming that the principle of restitution for theft persists into the Kingdom of God (Luke 19:9).

Additional restitution is required when a capital good is stolen. An ox can be used to pull a plough or sledge, so it is a capital good that will produce a stream of income into the future. Stealing an ox makes the owner less productive for the lifetime of the oxen. Using a modern example, the theft of a carpenter's tools (his capital goods) costs him more than the theft of something he has made. The Laws for Society specify fivefold-restitution for the theft of capital goods.

Under modern justice, fines are paid to the state, so the victim receives nothing. If the criminal is sent to prison, innocent citizens pay the cost and the victim still misses out. Under the Laws for Society, the victim is compensated for their loss.

Detecting Thieves

The compensation a victim receives will be sufficient to pay for the cost of tracking down the thief. This gives power to the victim. In the modern system, the victim of theft has to rely on the police to track down the criminal. If theft is not a priority for the police, nothing will happen. Under the Laws for Society, the victim can pay someone to track down the thief, knowing that the restitution they will receive will cover the cost. The victim has control over the action taken.

People with detective skills might track down thieves on the condition that they are paid, if they get a conviction. Provided they get a conviction for about half of the crimes they investigate, they will be able to recover their costs from their clients. God's Laws for Society give citizens control over justice. They can choose the best detective in their neighbourhood.

Bonded Employment

For financial restitution to be effective, a process is needed for people who cannot afford it. If poor people are not required to make restitution, they will be able to break the law with impunity. The biblical solution is the "restitution loan". A convicted thief would get a family member or neighbour to lend them the money to make the restitution payment.

A restitution loan would usually be interest free (Lev 25:36). The thief would be bonded to the lender to guarantee the repayment of the loan. While under the bond, they would be provided money to cover food and shelter, but the rest of their earnings would go to repaying the loan (Ex 22:3). They would have to stay close to their place of work and be unable to travel without permission from the person who made the loan.

The term of the bond would depend on the amount of the restitution. If the items stolen were valuable, the restitution might be quite large, so the thief might lose their freedom for several years. The term would also depend on the productive capacity of the thief. Unlike a charity loan to someone who falls into poverty, the debt would not be cancelled after seven years (Ex 21:2).

The Laws of Society provide strong protections for "bonded employees". If they are mistreated, they can go before a judge and claim their freedom as compensation (Ex 21:26-27; Deut 15:12-18). This gives employers a strong economic incentive to treat their bonded employees fairly.

A bonded employee has an incentive to work hard and learn new skills. By becoming more productive for their employer, they might be able to negotiate an earlier release from the bond. Developing good work habits and increasing their earning power would make them less likely to offend in the future.

Mercy
Judges should exercise mercy when deciding the remedy for theft.

> Mercy triumphs over justice (James 2:13).

The judge should take into account the circumstances of the thief and be careful about punishing innocent children. Their aim must be the restoration of both the thief and their victim, so the biblical remedies for theft must be tempered with mercy.

Full fourfold restitution would only be demanded in the more serious cases. If it is a second or third offence, and the person tries to cover up their dishonesty, or tries to evade justice, a stiffer penalty might be required. However, if the thief is young and remorseful, and it is their first offence, returning the stolen property, or paying the cost of its replacement, might be sufficient to get them back to a better life. Followers of Jesus will usually turn the other cheek and forgo restitution.

Free to flee
Judges do not have authority to restrain a thief, so they will be able to flee rather than pay the specified restitution. Some people will refuse to recognise authority of local judges and run away when they are challenged to put things right. Of course, they will not be welcome in many other Kingdom Communities when it is heard that they are unrepentant. They might need to flee to a less desirable community to find acceptance.

If the thief flees, or is not found, the elders of the community will ensure that the victims of the thief do not suffer. They will urge the citizens of the Kingdom Community to give generously to the victims of injustice. They will receive their restitution indirectly through the body of Jesus.

Some people coming to faith in Jesus will be owners of "unrighteous wealth". The Holy Spirit will convict some of them about their wealth and prompt them to make restitution to the people they harmed.

Sometimes they will have lost contact with the victims of their unrighteousness. If the unrighteousness occurred several generations back, they would not even know who they were. They will give their "unrighteous wealth" to those in need within their Kingdom Community. Many of Zacchaeus's victims did not even know they had paid too much tax, so he gave half his wealth to the poor (Luke 19:8).

In a Kingdom Community, money will flow from those holding "unrighteous wealth" to those who have been victims of crime and injustice. This will often replace direct restitution as a vehicle of justice (more on unrighteous wealth in chapter 12).

False Witness
False witness includes perjury, fraud, defamation of character, broken contracts and broken covenants. The remedy for perjury is the penalty that would have been received by the person falsely accused.

> If a malicious witness takes the stand to accuse a man of a crime, the two men involved in the dispute must stand in the presence of the Lord before the priests and the judges who are in office at the time. The judges must make a thorough investigation, and if the witness proves to be a liar, giving false testimony against his brother, then do to him as he intended to do to his brother. You must purge the evil from among you (Deut 19:16-19).

Defamation robs a person's reputation, so the defamed person is entitled to restitution for their loss. Fraud and broken contracts are also forms of theft, so restitution is the appropriate remedy.

Assault

The restoration principle also applies to assault. The person who has assaulted another must compensate their victim for the harm they have done to them, including damage to their property. A practical example is given in the following verses.

> If men quarrel and one hits the other with a stone or with his fist and he does not die but is confined to bed, the one who struck the blow will not be held responsible, if the other gets up and walks around outside with his staff; however, he must pay the injured man for the loss of his time and see that he is thoroughly healed (Ex 21:18-19).

The person who assaults another must compensate their victim for any income lost. They must also pay for the full cost of restoring the victim to health. The word health is repeated in the Hebrew text for emphasis (healed to health). If the victim cannot be restored to health, they must be compensated for any permanent loss.

The expression "an eye for an eye" is well known, but is totally misunderstood. Almost everyone assumes that the Laws for Society specify physical revenge for personal injuries. "Eye for an eye" is not a physical punishment, but a method for deciding financial compensation.

The law confirms that the purpose of the "eye for eye" principle is almost totally opposite to the popular view.

> If men who are fighting hit a pregnant woman and she gives birth prematurely but there is no serious injury, the offender must pay whatever the woman's husband demands and the court allows. And if any harm follows, the offender must give life for life, eye for eye, tooth for tooth, hand for hand, foot for foot, burn for burn, wound for wound, bruise for bruise (Ex 21:22-25).

The passage specifies financial compensation for the loss of the baby and not physical vengeance. In this situation, two men fighting have hit a pregnant woman so that she gives premature birth. The mother is entitled to the financial compensation demanded by her husband and approved by a court. "An eye for an eye" is nothing more than a principle for deciding the value of the economic restitution that the violent man must pay his victim.

Judges should decide on the appropriate financial compensation by assessing the economic value of the damaged limb or organ. They must estimate the value of the income and enjoyment lost because of the injury. This is like the lump-sum compensation provided by some accident insurance schemes.

God could not define just compensation in terms of shekels, because inflation changes the value of a currency over time. By linking compensation back to the value of a limb or organ, God provided a compensation principle that is relevant in every culture, regardless of the currency.

Jesus Clarified

Jesus dealt with this issue in the Sermon on the Mount. In his time, the "eye for an eye principle" was being used as a justification for physical revenge. Jesus rejected this as a distortion of the law.

> You have heard that it was said… but I say to you (Matt 5:38).

Jesus distanced himself from the popular interpretation because he knew that the Law prohibited all forms of revenge.

> Do not seek revenge or bear a grudge… but love your neighbour as yourself. I am the Lord (Lev 19:18).

Jesus rejected the popular justification for revenge and reminded his listeners of another popular saying that twisted God's law.

> You have heard that it was said, "Love your neighbour and hate your enemy." But I tell you, "love your enemies and pray for those who persecute you" (Matt 5:43).

Jesus knew the Law did not tell people to hate their enemies, but required them to love their neighbours regardless of what they did (Lev 19:18). It does not justify hating or harming enemies.

People had twisted "An eye for an eye" into an excuse for revenge. This was a distortion of God's law, which specified a method for determining appropriate financial compensation.

Modern justice makes offenders pay fines to the government, but very rarely provides financial compensation to the victims of violence. The Laws of Society provide compensation to the victims of violence. God's justice is better than human law.

Murder

Murder should be rare in Kingdom Communities, because murder is a failure of spiritual protection. A person who murders another has been taken over by spirits of anger, hatred and violence, so if a Kingdom Community has strong spiritual protection, murder should be very rare.

The Laws for Society specifies "life for life" as the penalty for murder (Ex 21:23) but we must be careful about assuming that we know what it means. "Life for life" is God's judgment on murder. Humans were created in the image of God, so killing a person is like striking at the image of God. Human life is so valuable that the person who deliberately destroys a human life deserves death.

A murderer deserves to die, but that does not settle the matter. God is compassionate and gracious, slow to anger, abounding in love and faithfulness (Psalm 86:15) so his justice is always merciful. He showed how to be merciful towards those who deserve to die in the Garden of Eden. God had warned Adam that he would die if he ate from the tree of the knowledge of good and evil.

> You must not eat from the tree of the knowledge of good and evil, for when you eat from it you will *die death* (Gen 2:17).

The word die is doubled in the Hebrew, as "die death". However, God did not put Adam and Eve to death when they ate the fruit. That is what they deserved, but he is merciful, so he excluded them from the garden instead. Adam lived on for hundreds of years, but he was shut out from the presence of God.

God implemented his penalty of "die death" as "exclusion". In a sense, Adam and Eve were dead. Their relationship with God had died. They lost their place of safety and were thrust into a dangerous world dominated by the spiritual powers of evil.

The same doubling of the word death (die death) is used in Exodus 21:12 to describe the penalty for murder.

> Anyone who fatally strikes a person shall *die death*.

Excellent judges should not apply this expression more literally than God does. If he implemented Adam and Eve's penalty as exclusion, the same penalty should apply for murder.

Exodus 21:12 is a statement of about what murder deserves, not a penalty that judges should implement. A murderer deserves death, but they should not be killed, as that would be doing evil to achieve good. Instead, the murderer should be excluded from their community. Their relationship with the community that had sustained them would be dead. They would be cut off from the people they trusted for protection, and exposed to spiritual attack.

Community Exclusion

A person found guilty of murder will be excluded from the Kingdom Community. They will be allowed to escape, provided they agree not to return. Most will have fled immediately after committing their crime.

The fleeing murderer would be choosing a desolate life. They would be cutting themselves off from people who have trusted and supported them. All the privileges and blessings that came from being part of a Kingdom Community would be lost.

Loss of spiritual protection would be the most devastating consequence. The spiritual powers of evil would take advantage of the murderer's isolation and attack mercilessly.

The reputation of the fleeing murderer would go before them and make them unwelcome in most communities. They might need to go and live with other criminals on the edge of society. Their new life would be very insecure, because they would never know when a vengeful person might try to harm them.

Limits on Exclusion

The Laws for Society place three limitations on the exclusion of serious criminals.

1. Accidental Death

The Laws for Society distinguishes between murder and accidental death. The intention of the person causing the death determines the difference. If the death was not planned in advance, it is assumed to be accidental.

> Anyone who strikes a man that dies deserves death. However, if he does not do it intentionally, but powers of evil let it happen, he is to flee to a place I will designate (Ex 21:12-14).

Murder has not occurred, so exclusion is not required. The Law gives guidelines for identifying an accidental death.

> If he impulsively pushes someone without enmity, or he throws something that unintentionally hits someone, or drops something heavy and it hits and kills someone he didn't even know was there, and there was not enmity between them, the community is to judge between the killer and his family using these guidelines (Num 35:22-24).

If the person did not intend to cause death, it should be treated as accidental.

The person causing death by their carelessness might need to flee for their own safety. People who do not respect God's law might try to take revenge. Specific Kingdom Communities might become a safe place by welcoming and providing refuge for people who have committed manslaughter.

2. Ransom

The Laws for Society allow a person sentenced to exclusion for murder to pay a ransom to their victim's family in return for being permitted to stay in their community.

> If payment is demanded, he may redeem his life by the payment of whatever is demanded (Ex 21:30).

In most cases, the victim's family will prefer a ransom, as they would benefit economically, whereas the exclusion of the murderer would bring them no economic benefit. The rest of the community would only be able to overrule their wishes, if the murderer continued to be a serious threat to other people.

The judges would decide the value of the ransom in agreement with the victims of the murder (or their family). The value of the ransom should approximate the discounted value of the victim's future earnings. If the criminal could not afford the required ransom, they would need to borrow the money from their family. If their family could not help, they would need to offer themselves as a "bonded employee" to a person in the community who could pay the ransom on their behalf. They would have to work for that person until the loan had been re-paid.

The ransom is an instrument of mercy, but it is not an easy option. The seven-year limit for charity loans would not apply to someone borrowing to pay a ransom in lieu of exclusion, so the offender might have to work as a bonded servant for most of their life. They would not be able to travel away from their place of work, but this is more merciful than the modern practice of imprisoning people for life.

Very evil people who are a risk to society would not be allowed to pay a ransom to remain in their community.

> Do not accept a ransom for the life of a murderer, who is
> really wicked. He must surely die death (Num 35:31).

Ransom is not an option for some murderers. The Hebrew word "rasha" is missing from many English translations. It means "wicked". Murderers who are unrepentant and staunch in their wickedness should not be allowed to pay a ransom, as they are a danger to their community.

Some repeat offenders are so incorrigible that society needs to be protected from them. Locking them up for a lifetime is cruel and costly, so excluding them is a kinder way to protect the community. When a person has become so evil that they cannot live in society, sending them away is a more practical solution.

3. Young Person

A young person should not be excluded from their community without the consent of both parents. Parents have the power to override the decision of the judges if they are willing to take responsibility for remedying the harm their son or daughter has done. This recognises the reality that young people can make serious mistakes, but still turn out fine.

On the other hand, if his parents agree that the young person is hopelessly rebellious, the sentence of the judges should apply.

> If a man has a stubborn and rebellious son who does not
> obey his father and mother and will not listen to them when
> they discipline him, his father and mother shall take hold of
> him and bring him to the elders at the gate of his town. They
> shall say to the elders, "This son of ours is stubborn and
> rebellious. He will not obey us" (Deut 21:18-20).

If a son is so stubborn and rebellious that his mother and father give up all hope for him, he should be excluded from the community, before he does more harm. If his parents believe that there is hope for the youth, he must be given another chance. If they think that he is redeemable, he must be given an opportunity to repent and remain.

Gracious Gift

God's Laws for Society provide a simple way for a community to restrain violence and theft.

- Restitution is the best way to deal with theft. A group of people can protect themselves from theft by requiring anyone from their community who is caught stealing to make fourfold or fivefold restitution. The victim of theft is compensated, so they are not discouraged from productive activity. Thieves will be discouraged by the cost of paying restitution.

- The law also provided a solution for violence. If someone assaulted a member of the community, they would be required to compensate the victim financially for any damage done (Ex 21:18-19). This compensation would include any loss of income for the victim and their family. Violent people will be restrained, because the consequences of violence would be costly.

Residents and Citizens

Restitution is God's standard for residents of Kingdom Communities. They are entitled to receive restitution as compensation for loss due to theft and violence. Their motives should not be challenged.

The standard for citizens of the Kingdom Community is higher. They are motivated by the law of love, so they will often respond to injustice with forgiveness and blessing. Love will prefer peace through reconciliation to restoration through restitution. Citizens will only request restitution, if their elders agree that the thief will not benefit from mercy, but should face the consequences of their actions.

Be Content

I have described how justice should function in a Kingdom Community, but restoration will not always be possible. Sometimes, wicked people will rise up, evil will prevail, and peace will not be restored. Followers of Jesus should always respond with love and service, even in the face of suffering and loss.

The Holy Spirit can turn loss into blessing, but there are no guarantees. Paul reminds us that we should be content in Jesus, whatever the outcome.

> I know what it is to be in need, and I know what it is to have plenty. I have learned the secret of being content in any and every situation, whether well fed or hungry, whether living in plenty or in want. I can do all this through him who gives me strength (Phil 4:12-13).

11

Voluntary Justice

No Coercion

In the Kingdom of God, justice is voluntary. This idea will seem strange to people who expect justice to be imposed by force. Modern judges have authority to impose fines and prison sentences. Their verdicts are backed by the coercive power of the government. This is Imposed Authority.

The Government of God relies on Free Authority. God will not impose his authority on unwilling people, so local judges only have authority over people who freely submit to them, because they trust their wisdom. They cannot use Imposed Authority to enforce their decisions on unwilling people.

Judges can hear the cases brought before them, but they cannot force people to appear before them. If an accused person refuses to appear, the judge cannot force them. All they can do is hear the testimonies of the witnesses and announce their verdict.

The Laws for Society do not allow people to be imprisoned as a punishment. Judges can specify the amount of financial restitution to be paid for a crime, but they cannot impose prison sentences. Prisons have no place in God's system of justice.

Under God's law, the authority of judges is limited to declaring a verdict and specifying restitution. Judges do not have power to enforce their verdicts. A person declared guilty by a judge can reject the verdict, or they can accept their guilt, but refuse to make the restitution specified by the judge. God's commitment to Free Authority means that Kingdom Communities need ways of implementing the verdicts of judges that do not depend on force and coercion.

Free Authority

The Free Authority of the leaders of a Kingdom Community is the key to voluntary justice. Everyone participating in a Kingdom Community is expected to submit to the love and wisdom of its leaders. In return for the privileges and blessings that come from belonging to the community, they are expected to acknowledge the authority of the elders.

Participation in a Kingdom Community is voluntary, but the condition for belonging is acceptance of the leader's authority. Freedom is not reduced, because the person is free to stop submitting and participating in their community. They would lose the benefits of belonging, but are always free to withdraw.

Free submission to elders makes a voluntary system of law and local judges effective. Willingness to submit disputes to judges and compliance with their verdicts will also be a condition for participating in the community.

When a person is accused of theft of violence, the elders will encourage the victims and the person accused to submit to one of the judges that are recognised within the community. They would urge them to get the dispute sorted, so that peace is not fractured. The elders would say something like this.

> This accusation could be true. We want people living here to be at peace with each other, so we want you to submit to a judge and get things sorted. If you do not like the judge your accuser has proposed, we will find one we agree is reliable and honest. If you refuse to submit to a judge, you will lose your credibility in the community.

The elders will encourage the parties to the dispute to submit to a judge. If the judge declares that the accused person is innocent, the elders will try to protect them from further harassment.

If someone refuses to pay the restitution specified by a judge, their elders would say,

> This community is based on love and trust. If you want to remain part of us, you should make the restitution specified by the judge.

The elders would remind the person that God expects them to abide by the decisions of wise judges.

> You must act according to the decisions they give you... Be careful to do everything they direct you to do. Act according to the law they teach you and the decisions they give you. Do not turn aside from what they tell you, to the right or to the left (Deut 17:10-11).

When someone joins a community, they are committing to the general values that shape it. Those who are unwilling to accept those values will gradually drift out and find a society where they are more comfortable.

Voluntary Submission

People used to modern justice systems may find the concept of voluntary justice odd, but there are several reasons why a person who lost a case would freely comply with the judge's verdict.

- Judges with the gift of wisdom will make good decisions. If the person recognises the wisdom and the justice of the judge's decision, they will be more likely to accept it.
- If people are praying, the guilty person will be convicted by the Holy Spirit and agree to make the specified restitution. They will recognise they were wrong and make restitution to put the situation behind them.
- The family of the convicted person might pressure them to accept the judge's verdict and pay the specified restitution, because they want justice to prevail in their community. They will realise that in the next case, they might be the victim and want a decision in their favour to be respected.
- Other judges will support a fair verdict by refusing to hear an appeal. They will encourage the convicted person to accept the verdict and make restitution.

- The people of the community will give their judges moral support by talking about their wisdom and urging the parties to the dispute to accept it.
- Members of the community will support the verdict by refusing to share with a person who refuses to pay the restitution specified by the judge. They will gently remind the person of the benefits they have received by being part of a cohesive community and encourage them not to shut themselves off from this blessing.
- A person owing a debt to the offender might pay the victim instead. Most judges would refuse to hear theft charges against someone assisting with the payment of restitution.
- Prophets living within the Kingdom Community will challenge the person to respect God and his judges and fulfil the verdict. They would explain that a person who refuses to accept the decision of a wise judge has placed themselves under a curse.

    > Cursed is the man who does not uphold the words
    > of this law by carrying them out (Deut 27:26).

- Prophets will explain that a Kingdom Community provides physical and spiritual protection for everyone living in their neighbourhood. A person rejecting the verdict of a wise judge will lose their spiritual protection. Because they have rejected the authority of their elders, they will vulnerable to attacks by the spiritual forces of evil (1 Cor 5:5).

The elders of the Kingdom Community would not allow the victim to suffer, if a guilty person refused to pay the restitution. They would arrange for someone in the community to pay the restitution on behalf of the guilty person. If the elders who paid the restitution arrived at the criminal's house and explained that the money is owed to them, it would be hard to refuse payment.

A guilty person would come under moral pressure to pay the restitution decided by the judges. However, this pressure must be motivated by love and focus on the restoration of the recalcitrant person. Intimidation is not permissible. God's people must not make threats. Their goal should be restoration of peace.

Another Community

If the victim of a crime belongs to another community, their elders would come to the elders of the accused person and seek to resolve the issue. They would choose a judge respected by both communities. If they could not agree on a judge, they might choose two, one from each community. If the accused person refused to submit to this judge, the elders would say,

> This accusation could be true. We want to stay at peace with our neighbours, so we want you to submit to a judge, and get things sorted. If you do not trust the suggested judge, we will find one that we all recognise as being reliable and honest. If you refuse to submit to the judge, you will lose our support and oversight. We are not prepared to put our community at risk of attack, because you are unwilling to appear before a judge.

The accused person would choose to submit to a judge to continue participating in the activities of their community. Most people would freely submit to a judge.

If a person accused by another community refuses to submit to a judge, the leaders might hear the charge and make the required restitution themselves if they think the person is guilty. They would take this action to maintain peace with their neighbours. They would then try to find a way for the guilty person to work and repay what they owed. If the person refused to repay their debt to those who had bailed them out, they would lose the respect of their community.

If the community leaders decide that the accused person is innocent, they would provide the innocent person with protection from further harassment from the other community.

Outside the Community

In the reverse situation, where someone experiences an injustice at the hands of a person from outside their community, they would go to their elders. The elders would approach the leaders of the community of the accused person and say,

> We want to stay at peace with your community, so this dispute needs to be sorted. If you want to continue our relationship with you, we suggest that you encourage the

accused person to go before a judge whom we all respect.
We need to get this issue resolved.

The other community would usually agree to this request to maintain their relationship. Even if it were not a Christian community, the leaders would probably agree so that they could obtain justice for themselves in the future if they need it.

Trust between neighbouring communities will be important for their wellbeing. Those that refused to support justice might find themselves isolated and unable to trade, because they would no longer be trusted. When trust disappears, the cost of trade increases enormously, so wise leaders would ensure that justice is done when a member of their community is being accused.

Jesus urged us to treat others the way that we want to be treated.

> In everything, do to others what you would have them do to
> you, for this sums up the Law and the Prophets (Matt 7:12).

If communities apply this principle to their interactions, justice will be done between them.

Community Exclusion

When a judge declares a person guilty, the elders of the community should help the person make restitution. They should do what they can to help the person change their behaviour and live at peace with their neighbours.

If the guilty person rejects the judge's verdict, they are also resisting the wisdom of the elders who are trusted by the rest of the people living in the Kingdom Community. They are undermining people who have loved and served them. Their relationship with the community that had sustained them would be dead.

If they persist in their bad behaviour, they become a threat to the peace and security of the community. The leaders might need to exclude them from the community to prevent further harm.

The person rejecting a judge's verdict would be left out of all community activities. They will lose all the benefits that come from participating in its activities, including financial support and spiritual protection.

Justification

The ultimate consequence for refusing to accept the verdict of a judge is exclusion from activities of the Kingdom Community. The justification for this "exclusion" is provided in the New Testament.

> You must not associate with anyone who claims to be a brother or sister but is a seriously immoral person... Do not even eat with such people (1 Cor 5:11).

When a person persists in evil that actively harms other people, they should be excluded from the community's meals and other activities, especially if they claim to follow Jesus.

Jesus confirmed the process for settling disputes before judges in Matthew 18:15-17. The first step is to speak in private.

> If your brother or sister sins, go and point out their fault, just between the two of you. If they listen to you, you have won them over (Matt 18:15).

If the person who has sinned will not listen, the next step is to take the issue to a judge with the support of witnesses.

> But if they will not listen, take one or two others along, so that 'every matter may be established by the testimony of two or three witnesses (Matt 18:16).

Jesus was quoting Deuteronomy 19:15, a passage that describes the work of judges.

If the person refuses to accept the decision of the judge and rejects moral pressure from the community to put things right, they can be excluded them from community activities.

> If they still refuse to listen, tell it to the church; and if they refuse to listen even to the church, treat them as you would an outsider (Matt 18:17).

Jesus said that if a person refuses to accept the verdict of a judge, they can be treated as an outsider. If the community agrees with the judge's decision, the person rejecting it can be excluded from their community.

Throughout the scriptures, God's remedy for extremely serious sin is always exclusion.

1. Garden of Eden – Adam and Eve were excluded from the garden.

2. Promised Land –   The Israelites were exiled to Babylon after repeatedly rebelling against God.
3. Laws for Society –   Criminals who persistently refuse to make restitution are excluded from their community.
4. Church –   Christians who persist in sin that destroys the body of Jesus must be excluded from the body (1 Cor 5:11).
5. Last Judgment –   Those who have rejected Jesus will be shut out from the presence of God (eternal destruction) (2 Thes 1:9).

Exclusion should always be a last resort for very serious sin, as it is a failure of grace.

Spiritual Exclusion

In the age of the gospel, exclusion will be mostly spiritual (1 Cor 5:4-12). The person rejecting the verdict of a judge loses the spiritual protection that comes from belonging to a Kingdom Community and becomes vulnerable to attack by the spiritual powers of evil.

> Anyone resisting a good judge is rebelling against what God has put in place. They bring judgment on themselves (Rom 13:2).

The most devastating effect of exclusion from a Kingdom Community is exposure to attack by spirits of wrath and destruction (Rom 13:4). Paul described exclusion as "handing such a one over to Satan" (1 Cor 5:5) because it leaves them exposed to serious spiritual attack.

The person who rejects the verdict of the judge respected in their community is rejecting the authority of its elders. This withdrawal of respect eliminates the elder's authority to provide spiritual protection for them.

Spiritual protection comes through submission to elders who stand together against enemy attacks. When a person rejects the authority of their elders, their protection evaporates.

For someone who has been living in a spirit-free zone, the change will be dramatic, and dreadful. The spiritual powers of evil will enjoy attacking someone that they have not been able to get at while they were under the protection of a Kingdom Community.

The elders of the Kingdom Community will warn the person of the distressing consequences of loss of spiritual protection, not as a threat, but to save them from danger. They will urge them to avoid spiritual harm by accepting the judge's verdict and paying restitution to their victim.

Once they understand the spiritual impact of their decision to reject the judge's decision, most people will prefer to make peace and remain in their community. They will find a way to make restitution and lift the curse they have put on themselves.

Last Resort

Exclusion of an offender must always be a last resort. The elders making the decision to exclude someone from their community should be weeping as they make their decision.

The person who rejects the verdict of a judge and refuses to pay restitution should only be excluded, if they continue offending and become a threat to the community. Most communities would give a person several second chances before adopting such a serious remedy. If the offending is minor, the person might be let off, especially if they have stopped offending.

The exclusion option should only be used for serious crimes that undermine the strength of the community. Paul explained that selfishness and greed are not sufficient justification for exclusion from the community.

> I wrote to you in my letter not to associate with sexually immoral people—not at all meaning the people of this world...
> In that case you would have to leave this world (1 Cor 5:9-10).

People should only be excluded, if their persistent wicked behaviour threatens the cohesion of the community.

The elders should be motivated by love, so they will aim to restore peace in their community. In most cases, they will prefer to deal with the problems caused by the difficult person rather than take the sad and painful alternative of exclusion. To restore peace, they will arrange for any victims to be compensated by the giving and sharing of the community.

If the Holy Spirit is moving in a Kingdom Community, the need for exclusion should be extremely rare. Most issues will be resolved by the love and grace of the Holy Spirit. If the Spirit is not active, excluding a person would usually be pointless, as there must be deeper problems underlying the community that need to be resolved.

Voluntary

The exclusion process must be voluntary. A guilty person cannot be forced to change their conduct. If they want to continue in their bad behaviour, they are free to do so, but they must accept the consequences.

Under Free Authority, a person who rejects their judge's verdict can withdraw their submission to the leaders of the Kingdom Community at any time. However, they must understand that the spiritual, social and economic support that the community has provided for them is voluntary too. They cannot expect people to keep including them in their activities, if they are hostile to the ways of the community.

Community leaders do not have authority to force a person to leave their neighbourhood. If the criminal owns their house or has a long-term lease on it, they are free to continue living there. They will be free to interact with residents of their neighbourhood who are not citizens of the Kingdom Community. Of course, the support might be weaker, and spiritual protection non-existent.

The most that the leaders can do is ask other citizens of the community to withdraw from the immoral person and leave them out of their activities. They cannot force people to stop meeting with another person, so their decision to withdraw will only be effective if everyone in the community supports their assessment.

If the decision of the leaders is not supported by the rest of the community, the offender would still be able participate in some of the community's activities. If the leaders are uncertain about their support, they will be reluctant to exclude a person.

Outlaw Communities

Until the Kingdom of God comes in fullness, fleeing a judge's verdict will be an easy option. Many people will avoid the consequences of their behaviour by ignoring the decision of the judge and withdrawing from their community. Evil will be drawn to the world where it is at home.

As the gospel advances, more and more neighbourhoods will become Kingdom Communities. People with a bad reputation will have greater difficulty finding another place to live. Many communities would not welcome a person with serious justice issues. They would not want to offend a neighbouring community by harbouring someone who has rejected their justice.

Groups of people avoiding justice might come together and form a community of outlaws. These outlaw communities would be a horrible place to live, as the leaders would be those who have refused to accept justice. The strongest people would rise to the top, so the community would have only rough justice.

The outlaw community would be a dangerous place, so most people would stay away from it. Some Christians might enter temporarily to share the gospel and tough people might visit for trade. A few relatives might visit, but this would be risky.

Fleeing to a community of outlaws would be a frightening option. Most people would choose to avoid exclusion by accepting the verdict of the judge and their community leaders. No one would have to stay in an outlaw community, but they might have to comply with the verdict that they had been avoiding before returning to the community they had escaped.

Voluntary justice will allow many people who commit crimes to escape the consequences. Followers of Jesus will often suffer at the hands of ruthless people. Peter explained that they should be glad to follow Jesus' example (1 Pet 4:13).

A few serious criminals would choose to remain in a neighbourhood where a Kingdom Community has developed and make threats against people they hate. If they engage in war against the community, they should be defended against like any other enemy invader.

Preliminary Justice

Humans have a fierce desire for justice, but perfect justice is impossible on earth. Even in communities with wise local judges applying God's law, many criminals will evade justice. This is not a problem, because the Laws for Society have two purposes:

- Protecting the community from theft and violence.
- Restoring the situation of the victims of injustice.

The Laws for Society cannot produce perfect justice. At best, they provide preliminary justice.

The person who refuses to pay restitution to their victim can evade justice, but their escape is temporary. They will eventually stand before a perfect and powerful judge. Those who have avoided justice on earth will have to stand before Jesus and give account for their actions.

> We must all appear before the judgment seat of Christ, that each may receive what is due him for the things done while in the body, whether good or bad (2 Cor 5:10).

> God will give to each person according to what he has done (Rom 2:6).

All the evidence will be brought forward.

> Men will have to give an account on the day of judgment for every careless word they have spoken (Matt 12:36).

Perfect process will be followed.

Jesus has endless wisdom and perfect knowledge of the law. He has lived through all the trials of life on earth, so he understands the temptations that we have faced. He will be amazingly merciful.

> The Father judges no one, but has trusted all judgment to the Son, that all may honor the Son just as they honor the Father (John 5:22-23).

Jesus will be the judge and he will provide perfect justice for every person. All the injustices that have been done on earth will be put right. Victims of crime will only get perfect justice at the last judgment.

12

Relief from Hardship

Whose Responsibility?

Modern governments spend enormous amounts of money trying to deal with poverty. They tax the rich and give their money to the poor. These attempts have mostly failed. To be a credible alternative, Kingdom Communities must provide an effective remedy for poverty.

God's Laws for Society provided effective solutions for people who fall into poverty. Jesus affirmed these solutions and adapted them to support the advance of the gospel. The outpouring of the Holy Spirit invigorated them with love and mercy. The early church demonstrated its effectiveness.

> All the believers were one in heart and mind. No one claimed that any of their possessions was their own, but they shared everything they had... And God's grace was so powerfully at work in them all that there were no needy persons among them (Acts 4:32-34).

Mercy and Love

Care for the poor cannot be based on power and authority, but must be wrapped in love and mercy. Jesus expects his followers to show mercy and compassion to those in need.

> Blessed are the merciful,
> for they will be shown mercy. (Matt 5:7).

The fruit of the Spirit is love, kindness and gentleness (Gal 5:22-23). Mercy and love respond to need without worrying about the cause. People sometimes get into trouble through bad choices. Others make good choices, but things still go wrong. Some suffer from terrible injustice. Mercy provides assistance wherever there is need, regardless of the cause.

Mercy does not need to be very discerning. When there is a need, mercy acts immediately, regardless of the cause. Mercy does not stop to find out if the cause is bad luck, poor stewardship or injustice. It responds to need as soon as it appears.

Neighbourhood churches will help everyone in trouble, regardless of what caused their suffering. They will give to those in need without asking too many questions and imposing too many requirements. They will help people who have messed up their own lives by poor economic stewardship. The people helped will have to give account to God for how they use the gifts they receive, not to the givers.

Mercy will often be abused, but that does not matter because our blessing comes from giving, not from the righteousness of those who receive. People took advantage of Jesus all the time, so we should not be surprised if we experience the same. Jesus promised that the merciful will be blessed. The blessings on mercy will outweigh any pain from being ripped off.

Local Assistance
All assistance to the poor should function at the local level where the people are known.

Caring must take place within strong relationships. Followers of Jesus will not tell people what they need, but will listen to their concerns and serve them. They will understand their needs because they live amongst them.

Neighbourhood churches will be more effective than human governments in caring for the poor because they will be motivated by love and compassion. Human governments have the power to tax the rich to help the poor, but they lack the wisdom and compassion that makes the difference.

Kingdom Communities

A neighbourhood church will provide financial support for everyone living within their neighbourhood.

Followers of Jesus should be sharing their financial resources with each other. The next step is to commit to providing support for anyone in their neighbourhood facing poverty (Acts 2:45).

A neighbourhood church should be concentrated in a small area, so love and sharing can solve most of the justice and hardship problems within it. If the cost of support is beyond their resources, the followers of Jesus are spread too wide. They need to focus on a tighter area.

There will be no needy persons within a Kingdom Community, except those who refuse to be helped.

The elders and deacons will establish relationships with other Kingdom Communities to share support.

- Communities in the country will produce food to give to those in the cities.
- Communities in the city with surplus wealth will supply those in the country with the resources that they need.
- Relationships between the elders of different churches will be important for making people aware of needs and ensuring help goes to those who need it.

Equality is the Goal

The common view that variations in income and wealth are wrong is confirmed in the Bible. God's goal is equality.

> Our desire is not that others might be relieved while you are hard pressed, but that there might be equality. At the present time your plenty will supply what they need, so that in turn their plenty will supply what you need. Then there will be *equality* (2 Cor 8:13-14).

This goal cannot be achieved by taxing the income and wealth of the rich and giving it to the poor. This makes the rich angry, but leaves the poor still poor.

Jesus cautioned the rich people of the world against trusting in their wealth, but he did not expect them to rescue the poor. He does not force the rich to be generous. He gives responsibility for the poor to his followers, not to the rich.

God is not interested in compulsory redistribution of income and wealth. He will achieve equality by generosity and sharing.

> For I testify that they gave as much as they were able, and even beyond their ability. Entirely on their own, they urgently pleaded with us for the privilege of sharing in this service to the saints. And they did not do as we expected, but they gave themselves first to the Lord and then to us in keeping with God's will (2 Cor 8:3-5).

This is a radical vision. If Christians take hold of this sharing concept, the result would be equality. Giving and sharing brings poor people up, as richer people freely give down.

Generous sharing will be normal in Kingdom Communities. Extremes of wealth and poverty will disappear, as those with plenty supply those in need. While the trials of life create inequality, sharing will push the community back towards equality.

Voluntary Sharing

Caring for the poor must always be voluntary. God does not force us to do good, so sharing must always be a free choice. The main point of the Ananias and Saphira incident is that giving and sharing should be voluntary. Peter explained,

> Didn't it belong to you before it was sold? And after it was sold, wasn't the money at your disposal (Acts 5:4)?

This is an important principle. Ananias was under no compulsion to give anything. He should have been able to keep the full value of the property for himself without facing any condemnation. All giving should be voluntary.

Sharing must always be a free response to the love of Jesus. Christian love creates a radically different attitude to possessions. Instead of being something to enjoy, they become a gift from God to be used to strengthen the body of believers.

Compassion must be the motivation for sharing, not condemnation. Giving must be motivated by love and not by peer pressure. Demanding that someone share is always unacceptable. Giving in obedience to Jesus should be a privilege.

Relief from Hardship

Visible Witness
Sharing is important because it makes the gospel visible. Jesus promised that if his people love each other, the world would be drawn to him.

> A new commandment I give you: Love one another. As I have loved you, so must you love one another. All men will know that you are my disciples If you love one another (John 13:34-35).

> I when I am lifted up from the earth, will draw all men to myself (John 12:32).

The people of the world are entitled to look at the body of Christ to see if its members love each other. Love is hard to see in the modern world. Forgiveness and encouragement are often invisible to those outside the Church.

The best way to make love for one another visible is sharing possessions. In a world where riches and poverty are normal, a Kingdom Community with "no needy people" will be a very visible witness to the love of Jesus. In a world that is hungry for love, the best witness may not be a believer saying, "Jesus loves me", but a group of his followers freely sharing their possessions.

Simple Lifestyle
As neighbourhood churches get serious about sharing their possessions, a different lifestyle should emerge. People will still own property and possessions, but their attitudes should be different. They will choose a simpler lifestyle, not because possessions are evil, but because they are irrelevant. Kingdom Communities will be so focussed on what God is doing that they lose interest in the things of the world.

If the Holy Spirit is really moving in power, Christians will find it hard to be absorbed in a newer house or a bigger yacht. If the Lord is "adding to their number daily", "retail therapy" will seem quite boring. If there is great joy in the Kingdom Community, because the sick are being healed and paralytics restored, people will lose interest in owning more and more things.

Sharing will allow members of a Kingdom Community to live better than the rest of society, while owning fewer possessions.

Consequently, they will be able to spend less time working for money and more time serving the Lord. If they are called to work, they will be able to give more freely to support people in need. Sharing will free up resources for supporting the poor.

Caring Methods

Followers of Jesus should avoid poverty by working for what they need to live. Paul stated this quite bluntly when that those who will not work should not eat (2 Thes 3: 10). Each person should try to provide for their own needs and have enough share with those in need (Eph 4:28).

Caring for the poor is the responsibility of everyone who follows Jesus.

> This is how we know what love is: Jesus Christ laid down his life for us. And we ought to lay down our lives for our brothers. If anyone has material possessions and sees his brother in need but has no pity on him, how can the love of God be in him (1 Jn 3:16-17).

Jesus laid down his life for us, so we should also be prepared to lay down our lives for others by sharing our possessions. The body of believers in a neighbourhood should commit to providing financial support for everyone facing poverty. People who fall into poverty will be helped in twelve different ways.

1. Family Support

The primary responsibility for supporting people in poverty rests with their family.

> If anyone does not provide for his relatives, and especially for his immediate family, he has denied the faith and is worse than an unbeliever (1 Tim 5:8).

Families should provide financial support for each other. This duty of care extends to children and grandchildren (1 Tim 5:4).

2. Deacons

Some followers of Jesus will specialise in caring for the poor. The New Testament uses the word "deacon" for this role. Deacons will organise support for anyone in the neighbourhood who needs help, including those who have rejected the gospel (Acts 6:1-7). They will teach financial management to those who are struggling.

- Some unbelievers will give money to the deacons, because they will appreciate the work that that they are doing.
- If the neighbourhood is wealthy, the deacons might channel resources to other neighbourhoods where people are poor.

Deacons should be full of the Spirit (Acts 6:2-4). They will need the discernment and wisdom that only the Holy Spirit can give. They would have personal contact with those that they are helping, so they could quickly weed out those who are taking advantage of their generosity (The ministry of the deacon is described in Being Church Where We Live).

3. Giving Away Unrighteous Wealth

As the gospel advances, unrighteous wealth will flow from the rich to the poor. In the parable of the Shrewd Manager, Jesus makes a distinction between "righteous wealth" and "unrighteous wealth" (Luke 16:11). Righteous wealth is gained through hard work, honest trade and diligent investment. Unrighteous wealth refers to wealth obtained through activities that are contrary to God's will, particularly those that are unjust. Many Christians are compromised by unrighteous wealth.

- They may have accumulated it before they came to faith.
- Some will own inherited unrighteous wealth. It is still unrighteous, because the process of inheritance does not change its character.
- Some Christians are engaged in activities that produce unrighteous wealth.

The only way to transform unrighteous wealth is to give it back to the person it was taken from, or to give it away (Luke 12:33).

Jesus told his hearers to give away their possessions, because many of them held unrighteous wealth. Zacchaeus is an example of a new believer giving away his unrighteous wealth.

> Zacchaeus stood up and said to the Lord, "Look, Lord! Here and now I give half of my possessions to the poor, and if I have cheated anybody out of anything, I will pay back four times the amount" (Luke 19:8).

New believers will often give their unrighteous wealth to the deacons in the Kingdom Community to support the poor.

4. Daily Food Distribution

During times of crisis and in poor countries, deacons will organise a daily distribution of food for everyone in the Kingdom Community who is poor (Acts 6:2). Regular distributions of food may not be necessary during normal times, so the focus will shift to caring for widows and others who have fallen into hardship.

5. Interest Free Loans

When temporary hardship strikes, someone in the Kingdom Community will give them a generous interest-free loan to help them get started again.

> If there is a poor man among your brothers in any of the towns of the land that the Lord your God is giving you, do not be hardhearted or tight fisted toward your poor brother. Rather be open handed and freely lend him whatever he needs. Give generously to him and do so without a grudging heart; then because of this the Lord your God will bless you in all your work and in everything you put your hand to… Therefore, I command you to be openhanded toward your brothers and toward the poor and needy in your land (Deut 15:7-11).

Several important principles apply to loans to poor people.

- No interest should be charged on a loan to a poor person (Deut 23:19-20). The lender gives up the interest that they could earn if they put the money in the bank, so they are giving their interest as a gift.
- The poor person should be given up to seven years to repay the loan (Deut 15:9). We do not know the future, so we should not commit ourselves for longer than seven years.
- A loan that has not been repaid at the end of seven years should be cancelled (Deut 15:1). This removes the burden from the borrower. The loan gives them an incentive to succeed, but if they fail, the burden will be lifted. The person making the loan must be prepared to lose the entire amount. This is why Jesus said,

> Lend to them without expecting to get anything back (Luke 6:35).

- The poor loan will often be provided by a family member (Lev 25:25). If no one in the family can help, someone in the Kingdom Community should provide a loan.
- We must always show kindness and respect to the person in need (Deut 24:10-13). Charity often makes the recipient feel dependent and worthless. Providing a loan tells the person that you have faith in them and their future. This helps build the person's self-esteem and self-respect.

A loan gives the poor person an incentive to get back onto their feet. Most people do not want to be in debt. They will usually work hard to pay back the loan.

6. Restoring Land

If someone in the Kingdom Community is forced to sell their property, someone from the community should buy their land and hold it in trust until they get back on their feet (Lev 25:24-25).

7. Gleaning

Gleaning is another way that followers of Jesus can help the poor (Deut 24:19-21).

> When you reap the harvest of your land, do not reap to the very edges of your field or gather the gleanings of your harvest. Do not go over your vineyard a second time or pick up the grapes that have fallen. Leave them for the poor and the alien. I am the Lord your God (Lev 19:9-10).

Landowners were required to leave some of their crop for the poor to glean.

The person in poverty had to work quite hard to get the help. Gleaning is harder work than harvesting, because the easiest part of the crop has already been harvested. However, this hard work develops good work habits and contributes to the self-respect of the gleaner.

Rural gleaning is not practical for people living in urban cultures. The people within a Kingdom Community will look for creative opportunities to apply the gleaning principle to helping poor people by developing modern gleaning opportunities. They might allow poor people to use some of their spare stock or equipment to get ahead.

8. Supporting Widows

During times of persecution, families of husbands and fathers who are martyred will lose their physical support. A neighbourhood church will commit to supporting all the widows of martyrs living in their neighbourhood. Paul gave advice about supporting widows in his letter to Timothy.

- Help should be focused on those with genuine needs (1 Tim 5:3).
- Widows should be supported by their families, especially their children and grandchildren (1 Tim 5:4). They should only go to the neighbourhood church, if their family is unable to help (1 Tim 5:8).
- Paul advised young widows to remarry, so they get access to family support rather than remain dependent on the church for a long time (1 Tim 5:11-15).
- Widows receiving support from the neighbourhood church should devote themselves to prayer (1 Tim 5:5).
- The widows being supported by the neighbourhood church should be expected to make a contribution to their community. They should be known for their good deeds (1 Tim 5:10).

Most support will go to older widows who are unable to care for themselves.

9. Job Creation

Sometimes the greatest need of a poor person is well-paid work. Participants in a Kingdom Community can help the poor by becoming employers. Being an employer is costly and more risky than being an employee. The reason for unemployment is usually a lack of people willing to be employers. The government cannot create jobs. Only employers can create jobs, so the best solution to unemployment is more employers.

Christians have the wisdom of God and the confidence of faith, so they are well placed to start a business. If they already operate a business, they can look for ways to expand opportunities to employ other people.

10. Sharing Capital

Those who care for the poor must get capital goods into their hands. This will make their work more productive, which should increase their income. The prophet Isaiah looked forward to a time when every person would own their own capital.

> Every man will sit under his own vine and under his own
> fig tree, and no one will make them afraid, for the Lord
> Almighty has spoken (Mic 4:4).

If everyone owns some capital, they can provide for themselves.

The market will not produce equality of capital, because it tends to reward the most successful entrepreneurs by increasing their capital. Some people will accumulate capital as they make good decisions and others will lose their capital through mistakes or adverse circumstances.

The land laws of the Old Testament were designed to maintain equality of capital at a time when land was the main form of capital. If someone became poor and sold their land, it had to be restored to them at the time of the Jubilee (Lev 25:8-28). This ensured that the distribution of land remained roughly equal.

The people living in a Kingdom Community will find ways to share capital with poor people to help them take up new business opportunities. Interest free loans are a good way of transferring capital.

11. Bonded Service

Bonded employment is an option for very serious poverty that is too serious to be dealt with by an interest free loan. This will be common with a person who has to make restitution for a serious crime but has no family member willing to act as guarantor.

The poor person will bond themselves to an employer for up to seven years in return for a lump-sum advance of their wages.

> If a fellow Hebrew, a man or a woman, sells himself to you
> and serves you six years, in the seventh year you must let
> him go free (Deut 15:12).

The term of the loan will depend on the amount advanced and the productive capacity of the person receiving it. During the time that the person is bonded, they will not be able to change employers or move to a different place of residence. The employer would give them enough for food and shelter, but the rest of what they earn would go towards paying back the loan.

The employer making the loan is running quite a risk, because they do not know how useful their employee will be. They may end up advancing more wages than they can recoup within seven years, especially if they are generous. There is also a risk that the bonded employee might abscond.

The employer is also required to treat the bonded employee well. If the employer does physical harm to a bonded employee, judges can set them free from their debt (Ex 21:26-27).

When the bonded employee has repaid the amount of the bond, they are to be set free. The employer must be generous to the departing servant (Deut 15:13-18). The employer should help the departing employee get started in their new life. God will bless them if they are generous.

12. Establishing Justice

Poverty is often the consequence of illegal activity by powerful people and companies. Poor people often do not have the resources to do battle against those who would deny them justice before the courts. They often give up, when faced by a rich adversary.

Local judges applying God's law will bring restoration whenever the legal rights of the poor are being trampled. Judges deal with injustice. It has the following characteristics.

- Injustice begins with an unrighteous event. Justice deals with something that has happened in the past. The event that produces the injustice will be identifiable (justice is backward looking).
- Injustice is caused by human actions. A person or group of people takes an illegal action that harms someone. An animal cannot commit an injustice, but a person who lets a dangerous animal wander may have done something unjust. A natural event is not an injustice. An exploding volcano may cause terrible harm, but it is not an unjust event.

Relief from Hardship

- The unjust action will have harmed a victim or group of victims. They will have been injured or lost something that belonged to them.
- An injustice has two parties. One that did the action that caused the harm and the other that was harmed by the action.
- Sometimes the injustice will have occurred in the past. A person might be poor, because their grandparent had their land stolen.
- The human action that caused the harm must be contrary to God's law. An innocent action that does harm is not unjust. If a wheel flies off my car and hurts someone that is not an unjust action, unless I have been careless about my maintenance. Justice does not attempt to remedy accidents.
- Injustice is different from sin. All injustices are sinful, but not all sins are unlawful. Pride is a sin, but it is not unjust.
- Injustice usually involves a dispute about what happened and who is responsible. The judge's decision settles the dispute by declaring the truth and deciding who was responsible. One party will be vindicated.
- Judges remedy injustice by specifying a remedy that will restore the victim to the position they were in before the injustice occurred. If the harm cannot be repaired, the victim should receive compensation for what they have lost.

Justice takes time. Investigating the situation to determine if God's law has been broken must be done carefully. Even if the victim knows who has perpetrated the injustice, they may not be easy to find. Bringing the unjust person to justice takes time, whereas the needs of the victim are immediate. Followers of Jesus should show mercy immediately, and seek justice later.

The injured man was a victim of injustice, but the Good Samaritan did not try to obtain justice, because the injured man would likely be dead before justice was done. He bound up the injured man's wounds and took him to an inn and paid for his care (Luke 10:37). Followers of Jesus should not wait for justice, but assist suffering people, while justice is being established.

141

Be Prepared

Poverty is one of the more persistent problems in the modern world. Human governments have spent billions and billions of dollars on welfare schemes, but human solutions always fail.

God has provided clear wisdom and guidance for dealing with poverty. We will only eliminate poverty from the world when we do it God's way.

When human governments fail, and social welfare systems crash, God's people must be ready to step into the gap with massive giving and sharing. This will be a tremendous opportunity for demonstrating the love of God and sharing the gospel.

(The restoration of God's law and Local Judges will bring restoration to the economy. I will describe his more fully in a separate book called God's Economy).

13

Protecting the Community

God is the protector of his people. Our best protection is to trust in him. We are "protected by the power of God through faith" (1 Pet 1:5). We must put our trust in God, not in military force.

Spiritual Protection
God's people will always be more concerned about spiritual protection than physical protection. The spiritual powers of evil are a greater threat than any human attacker. Human armies usually attack communities that have lost their spiritual protection, so spiritual protection is more important than physical protection. If spiritual protection is strong, other forms of defence will rarely be needed.

Followers of Jesus will bring spiritual protection that benefits everyone in their neighbourhood.

- They will watch over each other and stand together in unity to resist the power of the enemy. They will enhance their protection by submitting to the elders watching over them.
- Other people in the neighbourhood may continue to sin and some may allow evil into their lives. However, none of these people will have authority over anyone else, so they will not be able to give evil spirits authority to work in their community. This limits the ability of the spiritual powers to interfere in the lives of others.

- The only people in the territory with authority over others will be elders. They will be submitted to each other, so their authority will be constrained.
- No one will be submitted to political powers and the spiritual powers that cling to them.
- The principalities and powers in the spiritual realms will not be able to get a stronghold in the community because political power has disappeared.
- A Kingdom Community will be an authority-light zone, so it will be relatively demon-free.

Risks to Peace

A community that relies on God's law applied by judges should be a peaceful place to live. Wise elders and judges will deal with threats to peace from within, but a prosperous community might face external threats. The leaders of a Kingdom Community should be prepared to deal with threats from outside.

We live in a hostile world. Although, the spiritual powers of evil are being pushed back by the gospel and the Spirit, they are also cheats. They will sometimes attack a community, even though they have no authority to touch it. They do not abide by the rules, so they will stir up people to attack the Kingdom of God whenever they can. A Kingdom Community will face a variety of risks.

- From outside, people following Jesus might appear to be prosperous, so thieves and burglars might enter the neighbourhood to steal from them.
- A person who has been excluded from the community might gather some angry friends and attack the community to get revenge.
- During tough economic times, gangs of youths might enter the neighbourhood to loot and destroy.
- The leaders of an outlaw community might decide to expand their wealth and power by invading Kingdom Communities in their vicinity.
- A war between rival nations might spill out and overwhelm the neighbourhood.

- A foreign nation might invade the peaceful community to expand the territory it controls.
- An expanding political empire might attempt to bring another region under its control.
- When an empire collapses, people everywhere will be distressed and vulnerable.

Community Protection

When the situation is unsettled and uncertain, local communities will have to provide their own security, because everyone else will be trying to steal it.

- The citizens of a Kingdom Community will trust in God for their protection. If he is not watching over them, all other efforts will be in vain (Ps 127:1).
- Protection comes from followers of Jesus being together (Acts 2:44). The early Christians protected themselves in a hostile culture by banding together.
- Citizens of a Kingdom Community will commit to providing protection for all residents of their neighbourhood, including those who have rejected Jesus.
- God's people will even protect those who are unwilling to contribute to protection efforts.
- The elders of the Kingdom Community will take responsibility for dealing with all threats to the peace of their neighbourhood.
- Residents will be glad to follow the directions of elders in a crisis, because they will be prepared, and know what to do.
- The elders will follow the example of Jesus and place the security of the residents ahead of their own safety.
- Safety of people will be more important than protection of property.

Prayer and Blessing

A community that is based on love and sharing would seem to be poorly equipped to deal with violence, but they are safer than those who rely on military force and Imposed Authority, because they rely on the power and goodness of God.

> God is our refuge and strength, an ever-present help in trouble (Ps 46:1).

> The Lord will watch over your coming and going, both now and forevermore (Ps 121:8).

Kingdom communities will rely on God for their protection from physical attack. Many evil people will be scared to go into a Kingdom Community in case God grabs hold of them.

When the people of Jesus face an external threat, they will take three actions.

- They will call on the Lord and ask him to place a wall of protection around their community.
- The adults in the Kingdom Community will gather together to meet the threat. They will pray for those who have come to do harm. In many situations, the presence and power of the Holy Spirit will cause the invaders to flee.
- The elders will look for ways to bless those who want to harm their community. If the invaders have come to steal, they will give them more than they could gain by stealing. At the same time, they will share the good news of Jesus.

Attacks by small groups of intruders will usually be resolved by sharing God's love. Those who refuse to be blessed will be confused by the prayer and disorientated by the offers of help. Many will disappear and look for easier pickings elsewhere.

Key to Victory

Our struggle is not against flesh and blood, but against the spiritual evil powers operating in the spiritual realm (Eph 6:10). A Kingdom Community that is threatened by an invading army is actually being attacked by the spiritual powers of evil that cannot be defeated by physical power.

Modern nations invest enormous resources in physical weapons to fight physical attacks, but this is wasted effort, because war is an invasion by the spiritual powers of evil. Evil spirits cannot be killed with guns and bombs. People who understand the influence of the spiritual realms will realise that relying on military force is not the solution.

Protecting the Community

Killing the people who are invading does not work, because the spiritual powers of evil that stirred them up are not killed. When their attacks fail, they become angry and will look for a better way to destroy the community they hate.

For example, if a group of youths attack a Kingdom Community, the people could resist them with their knives and shotguns and scare them into leaving. However, the spiritual powers of evil controlling the youths are not defeated, just annoyed. They will re-organise and return with stronger force.

The spiritual powers of evil hate being threatened or intimidated, because that is their game. They will always respond to threats with greater spiritual intimidation. They cannot be scared away. The only way to defeat the spiritual powers of evil is to defeat them spiritually, by binding them in the name of Jesus and forcing them to surrender.

The only way to stop an invading army is to prevent the spiritual powers of evil from entering the territory that the army is trying to invade. If the spiritual powers of evil are unable to cross the border, because people with spiritual authority in the territory they are attacking resist them, it is unlikely that the human army will enter. Soldiers will be afraid to attack, if the spiritual powers of evil are not cheering them on.

Moses defeated Pharaoh's army in this way. When he stretched out his hand over the sea, it rolled in and destroyed the enemy force (Exodus 15:6). When Sennacherib king of Assyria attacked Jerusalem, Isaiah prophesied against him. God sent an angel who destroyed the fighting men and pushed back the evil spirits that were controlling them (2 Chron 32:20-22).

When the Moabites and Ammonites attacked Judah, King Jehoshaphat sought the Lord. The Holy Spirit came on Zechariah and he prophesied to the people and told them where to stand. He reminded them that "The battle is not yours, but God's". Jehoshaphat appointed singers to praise God at the front of the army. When the song rose to the Lord, the Moabites and Ammonites attacked each other and destroyed themselves (2 Chron 20).

These victories occurred because the Holy Spirit prompted the evil spirits that had stirred up the invading armies to fight each other. This is how God prefers to defend his people.

Focus on the Spiritual

When a Kingdom Community is threatened with attack, the elders should seek the Lord and find out how he wants them to defend their community. They should do what he tells them to do.

God will usually tell them to engage in spiritual warfare. Their prayers will be directed against the spiritual powers of evil that are trying to invade their territory. They will resist them and prevent them from entering the territory where their Kingdom Community is based.

People of faith will stand together in the name of Jesus to bind the evil spiritual powers that are trying to enter their territory and command them to remain outside. If the spiritual powers of evil are unable to invade the territory, the invading soldiers will struggle to enter.

Prophetic people will pray that the Lord would send confusion among them, so they go the wrong way. They will release antagonism among them, so they start fighting against each other.

The Midianite army faced by Gideon filled the Valley of Jezreel like a swarm of locusts. Their number was too many to count (Jud 6:33). Gideon stood up against them with a revelation from God and 300 men, armed with trumpets and torches (Jud 7:7,16). They did not seem to have swords. When they turned on their lights and sounded their trumpets, God threw the Midianites soldiers into confusion and they attacked each other (Jud 7:22). This formidable army fled in fear.

War is always a spiritual attack, so it is the spiritual invaders that must be defeated, not the military forces. They are just a vehicle that the spiritual forces are using to be carried into the territory. God's people must wage war against the spiritual powers of evil, not the people that they are using to make their attack.

The key to defence is keeping the spiritual powers of evil out of the territory where the Kingdom Community is based. This is why a church should be concentrated together in a neighbourhood. If the followers of Jesus are spread too wide, it would be too easy for the spiritual powers of evil to penetrate. A Kingdom Community can only defend a territory that is small and compact.

War Zone

Prayer and spiritual warfare will defuse many threats, but there are no guarantees. A Kingdom Community will often be overwhelmed by military power. God will keep his people safe whatever happens. However, we dwell in the midst of a battle zone, and should live accordingly.

- Although they were defeated on the cross, the spiritual powers of evil are still engaged in a desperate but vain struggle against God and his angels. They love to stir up war, so they can kill, steal and destroy.
- Political leaders all over the world engage in war to expand their power. Many have stirred up nationalistic fervour to justify conflict. Politicians have much to gain and little to lose from war. When they win, war boosts their popularity and power, whereas the cost of the war is paid by the taxpayers and the conscripts who give their lives.
- Empires fall and rise. When empires are in their expansion phase, they will engage in war to expand their dominion. God's people will sometimes get steamrolled by these adventures.
- Kingdom communities will often be surrounded by people who have rejected the gospel. Angry people will sometimes covet their prosperity and decide to invade and steal it.

In many places, conflict and war will be a regular occurrence.

God's people do not need to defend their lifestyle with physical force. The gospel has often done better under persecution, so we should not be afraid of military defeat. We might have more opportunities to demonstrate his love. The survival of the body of Jesus does not depend on fighting, but on how we live.

Freedom is not an absolute value. It may be better for a Kingdom Community to lose its freedom than to lose many lives in an unsuccessful defence. The leaders of a community confronted by war should remember:

- Jesus has set us free, so political or military powers cannot take our freedom.
- Invading soldiers can kill our bodies, but they cannot destroy our life in Jesus. The worst that they can do is to send us to be with him.
- The body of Jesus was born in the Roman Empire and has blossomed under terrible empires.
- The advance of Jesus' Kingdom never depends on a war being won.

Our freedom comes from Jesus, not political independence, so it does not justify the cost of war. This may seem strange to the modern mind, but we can continue to serve Jesus, even when we are controlled by a hostile military power.

Submit to Invaders

If a Kingdom Community is invaded, the followers of Jesus should submit to the political powers that have gained control of them. Peter explained what should be done in these situations. Although the political powers that control them are not from God, they should submit to their power for the sake of peace.

> Submit yourselves to every human creation for the Lord's sake, whether to the king as supreme, or to governors... that by doing good you may put to silence the ignorance of foolish men (1 Pet 2:13-14).

Peter is not describing an ideal government, but is explaining how Christians should live under a hostile government. The emperor and his governors are a human institution. The word usually translated as "institution" is a derivative of the word for "create", so emperors, kings and governors are the creations of men, not the creation of God. The Greek word that Peter uses for governor is "hegemon". These governors are sent by the king, not by God as some translations imply.

Peter is a realist. Emperors and governors have real political power, so fighting against them is pointless. Since Christians have very little choice, they should submit to these kings and "hegemons" to gain freedom to do God's work. They might need to submit to political powers, but they should not confuse this with submitting to God.

The citizens of the Kingdom Community must submit to the human authorities that control them. They should not fight against their control, because that would be a distraction. Instead, they should focus on loving one another and sharing the gospel.

> Dear friends, I urge you, as aliens and strangers in the world.... Live such good lives among the pagans that, though they accuse you of doing wrong, they may see your good deeds (1 Pet 2:11-12).

As far as is possible, the citizens of the Kingdom Community will carry on living in the way that they lived before they were invaded. They will continue sharing their wealth, caring for the poor, resolving, disputes, offering wisdom and protecting their neighbours. They will continue to care for each other, and wait for God to set them free.

Tribulation Normal

God has not promised that he will always defeat our enemies. He has warned that in the world, we will have trouble and tribulation.

> In the world you will have tribulation; but be of good cheer, I have overcome the world (John 16:33).

Persecution is normal for followers of Jesus.

> Everyone who wants to live a godly life in Christ Jesus will be persecuted (2 Tim 3:12).

God has not promised to protect his people from persecution and tribulation. Those who are serious about following Jesus should expect them. He has promised to be with us, whatever happens.

> Who shall separate us from the love of Christ? Shall trouble or hardship or persecution or famine or nakedness or danger or sword? No, in all these things we are more than conquerors through him who loved us (Rom 8:35,37).

In any particular situation, we don't know what outcome will bring the most glory to God.

Sometimes God will throw the invading army into disarray and cause them to flee. He will give his people a great victory over the attacking forces.

On other occasions, he will allow the attacking army to overwhelm his people and seize control of their community. He will accomplish his purpose through his people taking up the cross and loving those who have come to rob and destroy them.

God can work through both outcomes, so his people must always be equipped for victory, but prepared for distress.

After telling his disciples that he would suffer and die at the hands of the authorities, Jesus challenged his followers:

> Whoever wants to be my disciple must deny themselves and take up their cross daily and follow me. For whoever wants to save their life will lose it, but whoever loses their life for me will save it (Luke 9:23-24).

Jesus was killed by the religious and political powers. Those who follow him should be prepared for the same. If a Kingdom Community is overrun by a military force, life will be tough for those who are following Jesus, but it is better to suffer for following his example than gain victory in the way of the world.

Vulnerable

Kingdom Communities will always be vulnerable. Some will be wiped out by political empires. Others will be crushed by gangs of ruthless people. Suffering is normal for those who follow Jesus. However, as they learn to love each other and stand together, we will see many victories, as God delivers his people.

14
Defence and War

Jesus' Way

God is powerful and wise. He can protect a Kingdom Community from evil attack. The previous chapter is short because protecting the community is God's problem. We just have to trust in him and do what he asks us to do.

God's people must not fight evil with evil, but overcome evil with good (Rom 12:21). We should bless those who attack us and pray for those who persecute us, and leave God to deal with them.

This approach is only feasible for those who are fully committed to following Jesus. This would not be realistic for communities with many residents who have chosen not to follow Jesus. People who have chosen to follow Jesus must not impose their standard on people who have not made the same commitment.

The standard for communities that are not committed to Jesus' way is provided in the Law of Moses. It was given when the presence of the Spirit with the children of Israel was sporadic, so the higher standard of the Sermon on the Mount was not practical. The Law provides God's standard for communities that have not received the Holy Spirit. Without his presence, Jesus' standard would have been too tough for the Israelites.

Turning the other cheek is only practical in the face of violence, if the people being attacked have the Holy Spirit working with them to resist the spiritual powers that are stirring up their attacker. Jesus' way is to resist the spiritual powers, but turn the other cheek to the person they are using to make the attack. The attacker is just a pawn in a bigger game. A loving response will disorientate the attacker and might weaken the influence of the evil spirits manipulating them.

Turning the other cheek towards attackers without the Holy Spirit working to disarm the spiritual powers of evil using in them is pointless. The Law is still the standard for communities that are not committed to Jesus' way.

This chapter is second best. It applies God's law to defence and war for people who want to use military force, because they do not trust in God for their protection. Until the Kingdom of God is fully come, this will be a common situation.

Second Best

Trusting God for protection from attack is hard. Some communities will not have sufficient faith to rely on him for protection from evil attack.

- Residents of the community who have not committed to following Jesus cannot be expected to trust God for protection. They will naturally want to rely on military force.
- If a Kingdom Community has fallen from grace and only a few people are still serving Jesus, the community might not have sufficient faith to rely on God to defeat the attacking force.
- If most of the residents of a neighbourhood have not yet come to faith, they will not be able to trust God for protection from attacks.

In these situations, the leaders of the community must not force them to do something that they do not want to do, as that would be Imposed Authority. They will most likely choose to use military force against a threatened attack.

Defence by Force

Although this is not ideal, God's law allows the use of physical force to deal with a threat of invasion. At a personal level:

> If a thief is caught breaking in at night and is struck a fatal blow, the defender is not guilty of bloodshed (Ez 22:2).

A householder can use force to protect their home and family, but it must be the last resort with the minimum force possible. If they are attacked while protecting their family at night and the intruder is injured, the householder cannot be convicted of assault. During the day, they would be expected to get help from other people in the community.

This is the standard for residents of a Kingdom Community. Citizens of the Kingdom Community should pray for the protection of their house and look first for a way to bless the thief. They should only turn to force when their love fails.

A person is justified in protecting their family from attack. If they see their children being attacked by someone evil, they should intervene to protect them from evil but should only use sufficient force to set them free. If there are several attackers, they might be wiser to call on neighbours for assistance.

This protection principle transfers to groups of people. The law allows several households to come together (as a Fifty or Hundred) to defend themselves from a hostile attacker. If a group of people use force to protect themselves and their families, they cannot be guilty of assault or murder.

Military force must only be used for defence, and only as a last resort. War must not be used to seize control of additional territory. The Kingdom of God is expanded by the gospel and the Spirit, not by military force. Military force must not be used to eliminate evil. That is God's job.

Voluntary Force

The use of force to defend a community from attack must be voluntary, so no one should be compelled to take arms and fight.

- Citizens and residents of a community must be free to choose, so people should never be forced to fight.

- Many citizens of the Kingdom Community will prefer to trust in God to deliver them, even though the threat is serious. Their choice must be respected.
- A Fifty or Hundred coming together to defend their community should choose people they trust to be their leaders and freely submit to their authority.
- Military leaders must exercise Free Authority. If they lose their respect, people must be free to withdraw their submission and choose another leader.

Dependence on a volunteer army will change the nature of warfare. Military leaders will not be able to order thousands of men to their death in pointless attacks as in many modern wars. They will go home, rather than continue a foolish war.

Counting the Cost

Physical force must be the last resort. Jesus said that before engaging in war, the leaders of a community should consider the costs and decide if they would be better to sue for peace (Luke 14:31-32). The situations where fighting an invader is justified will be extremely rare. Very few circumstances would justify the death and damage done by war.

The forces of the Kingdom Communities will be "fairly feeble", so war could only be successful against a very weak threat. Going to war might be justified if the invading force is small and could be defeated with minimal loss of life. However, a weak enemy will not usually risk attacking a stronger community, so this situation will be rare.

The full social and economic cost must be taken into account when counting the cost. The economic waste of war is enormous and the personal cost to the families of the casualties is terrible.

The spiritual cost must be included in the reckoning of the cost. War has a desensitising effect on its participants, and good people can be drawn into doing great evil that they have to live with for the rest of their lives. Men and women returning from war usually carry many evil spirits, because the fear and anger of battle give them a stronghold. The spiritual costs of war are so horrifying that situations that justify it will be very rare.

People counting the cost should note that war usually fails to achieve its objective. Even if the battle is won, it usually results in greater evil than the one that it was intended to overcome.

The spiritual powers of evil love war, because they enjoy maiming and killing people and destroying God's creation. When a small war starts, they smell the blood and rush in from all over the world. They even start fighting amongst themselves. What began as a small war turns into a great evil.

When an army invades, it is actually the spiritual powers of evil stirring it up to do evil. Killing soldiers is not the solution, because the spiritual powers of evil remain and can stir up others to attack. War often fails to achieve peace, even if the battle is won, because the spiritual powers of evil are strengthened.

If overwhelming forces are threatening to invade, military defence would result in serious loss of life. The leaders of the community should sue for peace, rather than engaging in a futile fight that would do great harm.

Jesus provides the best example of a wise surrender. He could have fought against the armed men the Jewish leaders sent to arrest him, but he chose to surrender. Some of his followers would have fought for him, but that would have done more harm than good. He knew that he could achieve more by surrendering and suffering on the cross.

War is only justified for defence, and defence rarely justifies the cost. In most situations, suing for peace will be the best option.

Feeble Forces

God's law ensures that military forces will be so feeble they are hardly military at all.

- Resources must not be wasted on making or buying weapons. In Samuel's time, the children of Israel did not have blacksmiths. They relied on the Philistines for sharpening their ploughshares, axes and sickles (1 Sam 13:20). From an economic perspective, this was unwise, but from the perspective of faith, it was perfect. None of the Israelites except Saul or Jonathan had a sword or spear (1

Sam 13:22). The Philistines had 3000 chariots with two
skilled soldiers for each chariot (1 Sam 13:5). Israel was
outnumbered in men and weapons, but this forced them to
rely on God for their physical protection.

- A community should defend themselves with what they
  have. The Israelites used the tools and equipment they used
  on their farms and in their households. Knives and
  hayforks were their only weapons. This prevented them
  from relying on their weapons rather than on God.
- Offensive weapons are forbidden in the law (Deut 17:16:
  Joshua 11:6), so artillery and missiles cannot be used.
- All military leaders will be temporary. They are given
  authority by local communities when a threat arises, but
  they must go back to their normal lives when the battle is
  complete. This limits their ability to fight wars, but it is
  better than having full-time military leaders advocating
  unnecessary wars.
- No money will be available for professional soldiers. Under
  the biblical model of defence, ordinary people come
  together to defend their communities. Wise leaders will
  emerge within the community.
- Participation in defence of the community is voluntary, so
  compulsory military training will not be possible (Jud 7:3).
- Voluntary defence teams will be mostly untrained. They
  will be armed with what they have. Their strength will
  reside in their unity and resolve, so it will be mostly
  symbolic. This does not matter, because God wants his
  people to rely on him for defence, not military force.
- Alliances with powerful nations are not allowed (Is 31:1).

These restrictions mean that the ability to engage in warfare will
be very limited. This has the following benefits.

- Military adventures to seize territory are not practical.
- Empire building is impossible.
- A community facing a military attack will usually have to sue
  for peace.

- If a Kingdom Community decides to resist the invader, they will have to rely on God's assistance. If God does not come to their aid, they will fail.

God prefers to work with weakness, because when his people are weak, he is strong (1 Cor 1:27). A weak defence gives him an opportunity to demonstrate his power.

Two Swords

Jesus confirmed the "feeble forces" principle when he faced a hostile attack. He checked to see if his disciples were armed.

> The disciples said, "See, Lord, here are two swords."
> "That's enough!" he replied (Luke 22:38).

The disciples had two swords. "Machaira" refers to a short sword or long knife that was better for defence than attack. It had many uses in a Jewish household, so it was not surprising that the disciples had a couple of them.

When Jesus said that two swords would be enough, he was applying the principle articulated in God's law, that his people should be weak in weapons, so they would rely on the power of God. Jesus understood the importance of spiritual power.

> I can call on my Father, and he will at once put at my
> disposal more than twelve legions of angels (Matt 26:53)?

Jesus did not need physical weapons, because he trusted his Father. He was committed to his Sermon on the Mount, so if he was attacked, he would turn the other cheek and trust in God. However, he knew that his disciples had not yet received the fullness of the Spirit, so they would not have the faith to follow his example. Therefore, he was quite happy for them to live by the standard of the Law and use force to defend themselves.

Jesus suggested that his disciples should have a couple of weapons in case they came under attack. However, he said that two knives were enough, because he wanted them to be weak, so they would be forced to trust in God. With two knives, a dozen men could protect themselves from a small gang of robbers, but nothing more. They could not deal with a bigger threat.

Once Jesus was confronted by a "crowd armed with swords and clubs" sent by the Jewish authorities (Mark 14:43), he counted the cost, and decided that he would surrender to them, even though they had no legal authority to arrest him. He told Peter to put away his sword (John 18:11), because he had chosen to die, rather than engage in a futile fight to defend his freedom.

Minor Threats

If the leaders of a community decide to defend themselves with physical force, the response should be proportional to the threat.

If the threat is minor, the people of the community could gather at the entrance to their neighbourhood to protect each other from attack. About fifty lightly-armed determined adults would be standing together in unity. Some attackers would think twice before taking them on.

A group of people who have worked with each other in their community will trust each other when resisting attack. Because they are defending their families and friends, they will be highly motivated. They would be able to protect their community against a minor attack, such as a small group of angry outlaws or a gang of rampaging youths.

Serious Invasion

If the invading force is larger, people from several communities might need to come together to deal with the threat to their society. People from four or five communities could form a Thousand to stand against the attackers.

- The elders of the first community confronted could send to the elders of other communities seeking help (Jud 3:27).
- A call to gather for defence should be initiated by the Holy Spirit (Jud 6:34). Gideon sent out a call for help when the Holy Spirit came upon him.
- Sometimes a prophet will call the people together for defence. When Samuel made the call, Israel had a great victory, because God thundered and threw the Philistines into panic (1 Sam 7:5-11).
- Groups of communities must only join with others to defend their society, if there is a good chance they will be successful without too many casualties (Luke 14:31-32).

- The strength of the relationships between the leaders of different communities will determine who comes together.
- Joining a Thousand must be voluntary. If the elders who receive the call do not think the cause warrants military force, they must be free to refuse it.
- No one should be forced to join the battle. Many will stay at home, because they do not believe that war is justified.
- The leaders of the Fifties and Hundreds forming a Thousand should appoint a temporary military commander.

Temporary Military Leaders

Military leaders are dangerous, because once they have tasted success, they can try to expand their power by engaging in further war. Accumulation of political power by military leaders is the most dangerous and most frequent consequence of war.

To protect against this danger, the role of the military leader must always be temporary. Once the threat is gone, the military leader must step down and return home. The following principles ensure this happens.

- Temporary military leaders are chosen by the people they lead. They are given authority when the elders of a threatened community choose a leader to lead their Fifty or Hundred and these leaders choose one of themselves to be temporary military leader of the Thousand.
- A temporary military leader is given authority when the people they are leading freely submit to them. This authority is temporary and voluntary.
- Imposed Authority has no place in the Kingdom of God, even when defending the community. If a temporary commander seizes excessive power and demands obedience, the leaders of the Fifties and Hundreds who have submitted should withdraw support and regroup under a better leader.
- If the temporary military leader is acting foolishly, the leaders of Fifties and Hundreds could take their people home. They will be friends from the same community, so they will be more loyal to their own leader than a temporary military commander.

- A prophet will sometimes identify the temporary military leader. Barak took up the role when a prophet called Deborah announced that God had anointed him to lead (Jud 4:6). The prophet will also challenge the leader, if they demand excessive power.
- Financial support for a temporary military leader should be voluntary and limited. This will ensure that they care for the people they are defending.

Moses and Joshua

Israel did not need a permanent military leader, because God had promised to protect them. Moses and Joshua took the military leader role until Israel had conquered the Promised Land. No successor to Joshua was appointed, because the role was unnecessary once they were in the land. God has promised to protect them and keep them safe from invasion.

Israel only needed a military leader when they lost God's protection by turning away from him. This happened frequently, because the people quickly became complacent and stopped trusting in God. He withdrew their protection and they would be invaded. When they repented, God would sent them a temporary military leader to rescue them (Jud 2:17-19).

Israel wanted a king because they had become dissatisfied with temporary military leaders. They lost God's protection so often, that they wanted permanent military protection, so they asked for a king like the nations around them (1 Sam 8:19-20.

Big Danger

When people rely on military power instead of trusting God, they are often tempted to make their military leader into a king. After Gideon had defeated the Midianites, the Israelites tried to appoint him as their king.

> Rule over us—you, your son and your grandson (Jud 8:22).

People assume that a successful military commander will be a good political leader, but that is not true. The ruthlessness and control necessary for leading an army in battle make a person unsuitable for leadership in most other situations.

The kings of Israel were permanent military leaders. Israel's rejection of God and his government created a permanent threat of invasion, so they needed a king to protect them. People who are loyal to God do not need a permanent military leader, because they become a burden on the people they control.

> This is what the king who will reign over you will do: He will take your sons and make them serve with his chariots and horses, and they will run in front of his chariots. Some he will assign to be commanders of thousands and commanders of fifties... and others to make weapons of war and equipment for his chariots (1 Sam 8:11-13).

The cost of maintaining a king and his court is enormous. The burden of these wasted resources falls on ordinary people.

A permanent military leader needs a professional army, but an army with nothing to do is dangerous, because it will get bored with training and want some real action (Deut 17:16). A permanent military force will be tempted to find situations where they can use their skills. They will push for war in every situation.

As the gospel advances, war will become less frequent. When human governments collapse and fade away, the major cause of war will be gone. The prophets looked forward to this time.

> They will beat their swords into ploughshares and their spears into pruning hooks. Nation will not take up sword against nation, nor will they train for war anymore (Micah 4:3).

Conduct of War

The defence of a community must be conducted according to the following principles.

- Before engaging in war, the leaders of the community should negotiate with the leaders of the enemy forces. They should be made an offer of peace (Deut 20:10). War must be the last resort, after much serious talking.
- The people defending their community must not attack and damage the land (Deut 20:19). The land belongs to God, so it is not to be harmed (Lev 25:23).
- People who have not joined the defence must be protected. Women and children must not be attacked.

- The defenders must not use offensive weapons (Deut 17:16). God forbade the king from acquiring great numbers of horses because they were offensive weapons primarily used for attacking other nations.
- Military alliances are common in the modern world, but these are forbidden again and again in the Bible.
- Once the attackers are turned away, the defenders must return to their homes. They must not attack another community. Defence ends when an attack is repelled.
- The defending army should make peace as soon as possible. Mercy is important. The victor should not seek revenge or reparations, but be generous in establishing peace.

Wasted Effort

If people turn away from God, they will be vulnerable to attack, no matter how large their military forces.

> They forsook the Lord, the God of their fathers.... because they forsook him …. In his anger against Israel the Lord handed them over to raiders who plundered them. He sold them to their enemies all around, whom they were no longer able to resist… They were in great distress (Judges 2:12-15).

Military attack is a sign that a nation has slipped away from God. The most urgent need is not defence, but making peace with God. Until God commits to the defence of the community, most military activity will be a waste of effort.

Jesus prefers his people to trust in him for their protection, rather than relying on weapons of war. It is usually better to suffer and die, than to go to war.

15
Voluntary Finance

Taxation

Modern tax laws give the government authority to take money from people without their consent. Political leaders claim that they need the power to tax, so that they can provide the people with things that they want to give them. However, this Imposed Authority has no place in the Government of God.

Compulsory taxation cannot be justified from the scriptures. Most people have not noticed, but the Law of Moses does not authorise compulsory taxation. The tithes to support the Levites and priests were voluntary. No penalties are imposed for failure to pay the tithe.

Render to Caesar

Jesus dealt with the tax issue when confronted by the Jews.

> They hoped to catch Jesus in something he said so that they might hand him over to the power and authority of the governor. So the spies questioned him: "Teacher, we know that you speak and teach what is right, and that you do not show partiality but teach the way of God in accordance with the truth. Is it right for us to pay taxes to Caesar or not?"
>
> He saw through their duplicity and said to them, "Show me a denarius. Whose portrait and inscription are on it?"

"Caesar's," they replied. He said to them, "Then give to Caesar what is Caesar's, and to God what is God's." They were unable to trap him in what he had said there in public. And astonished by his answer, they became silent (Luke 20:20-26).

This incident has caused a lot of confusion. The usual interpretation is that Caesar's image on the coin proves that he owns it, so it must be given back to him if he asks for it. This is economic nonsense.

An image on a coin proves nothing. New Zealand five dollar notes have a picture of Edmund Hilary, the first person to climb Mount Everest. To suggest that he owns every five dollar note is absurd. The coin that Jesus looked at belonged to the person who had given it to him, unless it was stolen, and then it belonged to the person it was stolen from. It did not belong to Caesar.

The image of Caesar on the coin was contrary to the second commandment. By putting his image on a coin, Caesar was rebelling against God. Jesus was reminding the people that Caesar was the enemy of God. They should not render anything to him.

Jesus urged the people to pay to Caesar what they owed him. Rome may have provided roads that were beneficial to their communities. I doubt that Caesar provided much justice for local people. He had not defended them, so they did not owe him much for defence.

When Jesus said to give to Caesar what belonged to him, he was not legitimising Caesar's taxation. He was simply restating the biblical principle that stealing is wrong. If the people had accepted a service from Caesar, they owed him payment. If he had taken more than he had given, they owned him nothing.

Jesus and the Temple Tax

An interesting incident occurred when Jesus came to Capernaum.

The collectors of the two-drachma tax came to Peter and asked, "Doesn't your teacher pay the temple tax?" "Yes, he does," he replied.

When Peter came into the house, Jesus was the first to speak. "What do you think, Simon?" he asked. "From

> whom do the kings of the earth collect duty and taxes—
> from their own sons or from others?" "From others,"
> Peter answered.
>
> "Then the sons are exempt," Jesus said to him. "But so
> that we may not offend them, go to the lake and throw out
> your line. Take the first fish you catch; open its mouth and
> you will find a four-drachma coin. Take it and give it to
> them for my tax and yours" (Matt 17:24-27).

Peter made the mistake of speaking for Jesus without checking
first, so Jesus had to put things right. He made two important
points. The first is that sons of are exempt from the taxes of
kings. Jesus is the true king, so the followers of Jesus are not
required to pay tax to earthly political powers.

Jesus' second point was that at times it is better to keep the
peace. He chose to pay the tax voluntarily to avoid embarrassing
Peter. His followers will sometimes choose to pay taxes to
political powers, because they do not want to get distracted from
their work for God. When they pay taxes, they are following
Jesus' example. They are not morally obliged to pay the tax, but
they will pay freely to avoid unnecessary offence.

Voluntary Subscriptions

Christian politicians do not usually take Jesus' teaching on taxation
seriously, because they assume that they will be unable to do
anything. That is not true. There are other ways that leaders can
obtain financial support without hindering human freedom. In
the Government of God, all attempts to obtain finance from the
people must rely on Free Authority. The best way is by voluntary
subscriptions.

A good way to fund local facilities and activities is to collect
voluntary subscriptions from the people who will benefit. Some
people will want the community to have the facilities even if they
do not want to use them. Voluntary subscriptions can provide the
local people with the activities and facilities they want.

I grew up in a rural area where most of the social, sporting and
cultural groups met at a public hall that had become dilapidated.
Many of the people in the district believed a new hall was needed.

A voluntary committee of interested people was formed. All the groups that used the hall were represented.

The members of the committee canvassed the entire district to get donations for the new hall. Some people would commit to a regular donation over several years. Many of the groups that used the hall made donations. When about half the money needed had been raised, a contractor was engaged to build the hall. A loan was raised to cover the remainder. The fees for using the new hall were set at a level that would allow the loan to be repaid.

No compulsion was involved. People not wanting to use the hall did not have to contribute, although some did. The money was raised by the people, so they decided on the style of hall they would build. All groups that used the hall were involved, so they got the facilities they wanted.

A whole range of local facilities and activities can be funded by voluntary subscription. The people will get what they are willing to pay for, rather than what politicians think they need.

Regular voluntary subscriptions are a good way to fund people who provide services to the community. In a Kingdom Community, a couple of roles might need regular funding.

- local judges;
- temporary military leaders.

All payments to both these ministries should be voluntary.

1) Payment of Judges

Being a judge will usually be part-time work, as most local communities will not have enough cases to occupy a full-time judge. Most judges should be able to earn their living by pursuing another career.

If a case is complicated and involves a lot of work for the judge, litigants might be requested to pay costs. The biblical principle is that a workman is worthy of his wages (1 Tim 5:18). Appeal judges hearing a lot of cases might need more regular support for their work. The person causing the case and the person benefiting would have a responsibility to cover the costs of the judges.

As the kingdom of God expands, the incidence of crime will decline and there will be less work for judges. Sometimes the people of a community might decide to pay a good judge a retainer so that they always have a judge that they trust available to hear cases when they arise. This would give the judge time to study God's law and keep up-to-date with decisions being made by other judges. All contributions to the retainer must be voluntary.

A risk to a society relying on local judges to apply God's law is that a judge might try to expand their role and try to remedy all social problems. The best constraint against judges expanding their power is their inability to impose taxes. The people can withdraw their support from the judge who gets big ideas.

2) Paying Military Leaders

When organising the defence of their community against an attack, the Temporary Military Commander might need some financial support. Most of the equipment will be provided by the men participating in the defence. They will be provided with food and equipment by their families, so the financial needs of the commander will be quite limited. Anything he does need will be provided on a voluntary basis by members of the communities under attack. The temporary military leader will not have authority to demand support, but will have to work with what is freely provided.

Once a temporary military leader has dealt with the threat to their economy, they should return to their previous occupation. Some will find this move hard, as giving up a position of authority is not easy. A misguided leader might decide to stay on to provide more permanent protection to the community. This is dangerous, because he can use force to impose his will on the people he is supposed to be protecting.

The best way to limit the power of a military leader is to limit the resources they control. Paying a military leader when there is no military threat is very unwise, because they can hire mercenary soldiers and become dangerous. An army with nothing to do often becomes a threat to its own people.

The best solution to this problem is to limit payments to the military commander and ensure that all soldiers are volunteers. If the military leader is dependent on the community for his resources, they can desert him, if he gets too big for his boots.

Just as payments to judges must be voluntary, military leaders should rely on voluntary contributions. A permanent military leader with authority to impose taxes can expand their power as much as they like and no one can prevent them. This will often lead to tyranny. Abimelech is an example (Judges 9).

Paul gives the principle for paying military leaders.

> If you owe a contribution pay a contribution (Rom 13:7).

People in the community should decide how much they have benefit and make a voluntary payment, so the temporary military leader does not suffer loss.

Allowing military leaders to levy taxes lets them decide the level of military protection needed by a community. They will often have an inflated view of the value of their services. Citizens must decide what value they put on military protection. If payments to military leaders are voluntary, they will have to persuade citizens of their community that their service is of value to them.

Most people freely pay house insurance to get protection in case their house burns down. In the same way, most people would be willing to pay a military leader to provide defence against threat of external attack.

Voluntary payments for military protection are the best protection against the tyranny of unruly military leaders.

Free Riding

The consequence of making payments for military leaders, judges and community facilities voluntary is that some people will refuse to pay. They can enjoy the benefits of the contributions of other people, while refusing to make a contribution themselves. A person who receives the benefit of being part of a community without paying is often called a free rider.

When the people living within a Kingdom Community decide to pay for something, free riders will benefit without contributing to the cost. The modern solution to free riding is coercion. This usually takes the form of a tax or compulsory levy. Free riding is eliminated, because everyone is forced to pay taxes.

Jesus had a different solution to this problem. When he died on the cross, he provided salvation for everyone who would trust him. We can receive that salvation without paying anything towards the cost. Every believer is a free rider on Jesus. He explained how we should respond to free riders in the Sermon on the Mount.

> If someone forces you to go one mile, go with him two
> miles (Matt 5:41).

The soldier who forces you to carry his pack for a mile is a free rider. He wants a service without paying for it. Followers of Jesus should not resist the free rider, but should show love him by carrying the load an extra mile. They should give more than the free rider expects.

Free riding will be a big issue for a Kingdom Community. The cost of community activities and facilities will often be borne by a few people, mostly followers of Jesus. The people living in the neighbourhood who have rejected Jesus who benefit from community activities will have no obligation to contribute to the costs. They will not even be obligated to live by Jesus' standards.

The followers of Jesus should not complain, because they are all freeloaders on Jesus' salvation. They will be glad of the opportunity to follow Jesus' example by blessing the people living amongst them. Jesus explained the correct response.

> But love your enemies, do good to them, and lend to them
> without expecting to get anything back. Then your reward will
> be great, and you will be children of the Most High, because he
> is kind to the ungrateful and wicked (Luke 6:35).

We must give, not expecting anything from the enemies of God living around us. Paying for free riders is a good way to love those who do not love us. Our reward comes from God.

We are all free riders on Jesus, so we cannot object to people free riding on us. When it comes to a choice between freedom with a few free riders tagging along and taxation with coercion, God's people should choose freedom and generosity.

God made us free, so we must not give up freedom, just to deal with a few free riders. His solution is not compulsory taxation, but love and generous giving.

Voluntary Way

If a group of people come together and purchase a water tank to protect their properties from fire, they could ask for contributions from those who will benefit. Many people would support the initiative and choose to make a contribution, but no one should be forced to pay.

Contributions must be voluntary. People who refuse to contribute should not be judged. Some will think the purchase is unnecessary. Their right to that view should be respected. Others may want to contribute, but be unable to afford it. Others who can afford it will deliberately decide to free ride. This is not a serious problem.

God's people should lead the way in paying for every service from which they gain a benefit. Some will contribute extra to cover those who cannot afford to pay. Others will pay extra to make up for the free riders. Compulsory taxation will be unnecessary.

People will only make voluntary contributions to community projects, if they support the vision of their leaders. If the leaders start doing things that are not supported, their finances will dry up. Before they can commit to spending money, the elders will have to persuade the members of the community to pay for it.

Avoiding Tyranny

Modern governments are powerful, because they have greater resources than any other institution in society. The power to tax gives the government enormous power.

If an individual or business takes something from another person without permission, they have committed a theft. Human governments get around this constraint by claiming the right to impose taxes and choose how they will be spent. Their ability to tax the increasing wealth of their subjects has given them enormous power.

Voluntary Finance

Making contributions voluntary is the best protection against tyranny. A government without taxation will quickly lose power. It will be very difficult for a ruler to impose control over a community without the power to tax.

Part 2

Uproot, Pull Down, Destroy and Overthrow

16

Uproot and Pull Down

Ten Big Roots

Modern political culture is dominated by ten institutions with deep roots in our culture. They will need to be uprooted and removed before the Government of God can come.

- Kings
- Presidents and Prime Ministers
- Democracy
- Legislatures and parliaments
- Political parties
- Taxation
- Political coercion
- Christian political power
- Revolutions
- Nationalism and nations.

None of the institutions on this list can belong to the Kingdom of God. This will be hard for most readers to accept, but the Kingdom of God cannot come to fulfilment while they are in place.

Kings, democracy and taxation have been part of our lives for so long that it is almost impossible to imagine life without them. They will have to be uprooted and removed before we can fully receive the Kingdom of God.

1. No Kings

When Israel asked for a king like the other nations, Samuel the prophet gave an important message about government. Every Christian who is interested in politics should study it. Samuel explained,

> They have rejected me from being king over them (1 Sam 8:7).

The Kingdom of God has God as king. By choosing a human king, they were rejecting God as their king. They were rejecting the Kingdom of God.

Samuel's message is clear. God did not want Israel to have a human king. He was their king, so they did not need a human king. A temporary military leader could be justified, if the nation came under attack, but a permanent king was not part of God's plan for his people.

2. No Presidents or Prime Ministers

God is king of the Kingdom of God, so citizens of his kingdom do not need a human king. On the surface, this does not seem to be a serious problem, because kings have become rare. However, presidents and prime ministers undertake the same duties as kings. They usually exercise more power than ancient kings.

Christians wanting a prime minister or president assume these roles are not covered by Samuel's warning, because they are democratically elected. This is not correct, as Saul was elected too. Samuel nominated Saul, but he only became king after his nomination had been confirmed by the people of Israel.

> Samuel said to all the people, "Do you see the man the Lord has chosen?" Then the people shouted, "Long live the king" (1 Sam 10:24)!

Their cry of "Long live the King" was a vote for Saul. David was elected in the same way (2 Sam 5:1,3).

Samuel's warning applies to presidents and prime ministers. There can be no presidents or prime ministers in the Kingdom of God, because God would no longer be king. Choosing to be governed by a president or prime minister is rejecting God's kingship and copying the nations of the world.

> No one can serve two masters (Matt 6:24).

We cannot pledge loyalty to Jesus and to political authority. Followers of Jesus who pledge loyalty to a president, or prime minister, or constitution, or parliament are serving two masters.

Declaring "Jesus is Lord" is easy, because the word "Lord" has no political content in the modern world. It does not conflict with pledging loyalty to human political powers. Saying "Jesus is President" or "Jesus is Prime Minister" is harder, because it becomes obvious that we are giving allegiance to two masters.

Presidents and prime ministers are modern day kings. They have no place in the Kingdom of God.

3. No Democracy

Many Christians assume that democracy is the best form of government, but they forget that it is rule by the people (demos kratos = people rule). Obeying the voice of the people is not obedience to God, so there is no room for democracy in the Kingdom of God.

Throughout their history, the people of Israel voted to worship idols and reject God.

> This is what the Lord says about this people: They greatly love to wander; they do not restrain their feet (Jer 14:10).

If Israel had been a democracy, it would never have made it into Canaan (Num 14:1-4, 26-27).

Jesus was crucified at the culmination of a democratic process.

> Wanting to satisfy **the crowd**, Pilate released Barabbas to them. He had Jesus flogged, and handed him over to be crucified (Mark 15:15).

The representative of an evil empire wanted to set Jesus free, but he put the decision to a vote and Jesus was sent down. Democracy perpetrated a terrible injustice by sentencing the only perfect man to death for crimes he had not done.

The crowd is usually wrong.

> Do not follow **the crowd** in doing wrong (Ex 23:2).

Our goal is the Kingdom of God. A system based on the will of people will not advance the Government of God. Democracy and the Kingdom of God do not mix.

4. No Legislature

God did not give Israel a legislative assembly. A law-making body was not needed, because he revealed his laws through Moses.

> These are the commandments the Lord proclaimed in a loud voice to your whole assembly there on the mountain from out of the fire, the cloud and the deep darkness; and he added nothing more. Then he wrote them on two stone tablets and gave them to me (Deut 5:22).

There is no evidence of a group of people being elected to decide on the laws for Israel. A parliament or congress was not needed because God had already provided a perfect set of laws.

Politicians can only make human laws. Those who seek the Kingdom of God should prefer living under God's laws.

> The Lord is our law-giver (Is 33:22).

God is our lawmaker, so we do not need elected politicians to write laws and regulations. God has given a perfect law, so we do not need parliaments and congresses to make laws.

5. No Political Parties

Factions, disputes and dissensions are rooted in our sinful nature (Gal 5:19-21). Political parties are well-organised "factions" so they cannot belong to the Kingdom of God. Political parties will have to wither away as the kingdom of God advances.

Many Christians commit to getting the "right" political party elected. All this effort misses the point, as political parties have no place in the Kingdom of God.

6. No Taxation

Although compulsory taxation is normal in modern life, God never commands payment of taxes. Compulsory taxation was introduced during a time of disobedience, when Israel rejected him and chose to have a king (1 Sam 8:14-18). Taxation is the outcome of disobedience to God.

God never issued instructions about taxation, because taxation is unnecessary when he is King. In the Kingdom of God, there will be no compulsory taxation. All civil or community activity will be funded by voluntary contributions.

7. No Coercion

God does not force people to obey him, but prefers that people do his will, because they love him. Forcing people to be good has no place in the Kingdom of God, so coercion is not allowed.

Modern political thought assumes that a government is needed to restrain evil. It agrees that force is evil, but claims that it is necessary to eliminate disorder. However, using evil to overcome evil is twisted, because evil always begets evil. We cannot overcome evil with evil (Rom 12:21).

8 No Christian Political Power

The temptation to advance the kingdom of God using political power is a powerful one, but it always fails because servant love and political power do not mix. A kingdom of love cannot be established by Imposed Authority. God advances his kingdom using Free Authority, so when the church uses Imposed Authority, it aligns with the world.

The people of the world assume that the Government of God will be like the modern governments that control every aspect of their lives, but with Christians in control. I am not surprised that they hate the idea. Modern state power would be dreadfully dangerous, if it were controlled by Christians.

9. No Revolutions

The New Testament writers saw Caesar as a usurper of authority, but they never suggested that the church should fight against the Roman Empire. Christians have often gone to war to advance the Kingdom, but these efforts have always failed. War usually makes a situation worse, even if the cause appears to be good.

Military power cannot defeat evil, because it always increases the influence of the powers of evil, regardless of who wins.
- When force is used against evil, the Holy Spirit is squeezed.
- When people rely on military power, the Holy Spirit flees.
- Whenever good people resist evil with war, spirits of anger and hatred are empowered.

When Christians take up the cross and follow Jesus, the Holy Spirit is released to establish the Kingdom of God.

We do not need to start a military revolution against emperors or parliaments, because our gospel is revolutionary in a different way. As more and more people repent and give their allegiance to Jesus, the power of kings and rulers will gradually leak away. The gospel undermined and defeated the Roman Empire, so it can destroy any political power. Prophetic preaching of the gospel supported by prayer will be more effective than revolution.

10. No Nationalism

Nation states are relatively modern invention, as five hundred years ago they did not exist. People lived in villages and their main loyalty was to their family and broader tribe. They might be loyal to a local leader who provided protection, but that loyalty only lasted as long as the protection. Urbanisation destroyed these local loyalties, so nationalism has become the glue that holds modern societies together.

The emergence of nationalism has dramatically changed the nature of warfare. War ceased to be a contest between kings and became a struggle between nations. Nations tend to fight over causes, and everyone is drawn into the struggle, which has vastly increased the destructiveness of war.

As the Kingdom advances, loyalty to the gospel will replace the false loyalties of nationalism. The spiritual principalities and powers that have used political power to control nations will be stripped of their power. We will all be citizens of the Kingdom of God and citizens of heaven.

Nationalism will be replaced by unity in Jesus (Gal 3:28). Allegiance to nations will fade and be replaced by loyalty to Jesus, families and local communities. Christ will be all in all, so nations will be irrelevant.

What is Left?

When these things are uprooted from our culture, it will seem like everything has gone, but two essential elements of social order will be left: law and judges. These are the foundation of a biblical social and economic system.

17

Destroyed and Overthrown

Every kingdom is based on authority. The Kingdom of God comes when his authority is acknowledged by everyone on earth. As I explained in the previous chapter, the immense authority that is claimed by political institutions will have to be swept away and handed back to God. This will be the biggest shift in authority on earth since Jesus died and rose again, so we need to know how and when it will occur.

Several big authority shifts have already occurred on earth. The next big one opens the season when the Government of God comes to fullness on earth. Unfortunately, the season will begin with trouble and distress that could confuse those who do not understand what God is doing.

The world will be ripe for the Government of God, but the people of the world will be fearful and confused. In this chapter, I summarise the flow of seasons through history, so God's people can recognise the next big authority shift as it happens. (A fuller description of these authority shifts is in a prequel to this book called Kingdom Authority).

Authority Created and Given
When God created the universe, he gave complete authority over the earth to humans. He retained his authority in the spiritual realms, but he gave authority on earth to the people he had

created. God was able to give authority over the earth to humans, because everything he had created belonged to him.

If humans had exercised their authority in obedience to God, life on earth would have been glorious. Unfortunately, this season did not last long, because Adam and Eve succumbed to the temptation to be independent of God. They thought they were gaining freedom, but they were unwittingly losing their authority. By submitting to the devil, Adam and Eve passed all the authority that God had given to them over to him.

From that day forward, humans have only had limited authority on earth, because the spiritual powers of wickedness had stolen the authority that God had given them.

- God continued to have absolute authority over most of the spiritual realms.
- The devil tricked humans into surrendering their authority to him, so he gained authority over the earth (Luke 4:6).

God gave humans authority over the earth without recourse. He could not demand it back, if they abused it.

Human sin shut God out of his world. He had the power to put things right, but he did not have authority to act, because he had given authority on earth to humans. He could only intervene, if humans invited him, but they had surrendered to the powers of evil who ensured that it does not happen.

God had a plan to save the world through Jesus, but he had to come as a man, because authority on earth belongs to humans in perpetuity. Only a human can legitimately hold that authority, so only a human could take it back. Unfortunately, Jesus could not be sent into the world immediately after humans lost their authority, because God did not have authority to prevent the forces of evil from destroying him before he had grown up.

Evil Expands

The next big season on earth was the millennium of darkness.

- God could only act on earth, if humans gave him authority
- Humans pursued evil and ignored God (Gen 6:5).
- God was shut out of the world that he had created.

- The powers of evil were free to entrench evil on the earth.

The powers of evil had more than a thousand years rampaging through God's beautiful world. The situation got so bad that the earth was in danger of being destroyed.

Humans love to point the finger and blame God for evil, but we gave authority over the earth to the powers of evil, so we are legally responsible for the consequences. We cannot shift the blame back to him.

After a thousand years of evil, prophetic people like Enoch and Noah began to call out to God. Their prayers and prophecies gave God some authority to intervene. Abraham responded to the call and established a people on earth who could give God authority to act. Moses led the people into Canaan and established a land where God was free to operate.

God gave Moses a perfect system of government, but the people rejected it and chose to have a king like other nations. These kings needed a hierarchy of administrators to control their people. This enabled the spiritual powers of evil to establish themselves as principalities and powers over the land.

Jesus

God's ultimate plan was to send Jesus to destroy the powers of evil and restore authority over the earth to humans, but he could not do this without permission from people living on earth. The declarations of the prophets gave God authority to do what he wanted to do through Jesus. This authority was confirmed by people like Anna and Simeon, who prayed for his coming (Luke 2:25-26,36-37).

Jesus' death on the cross was the biggest Authority Shift in human history. Human sin had given the spiritual powers of evil authority over the earth and its people. By paying the penalty for sin, Jesus eliminated the source of their authority.

Before he ascended into heaven, Jesus said something absolutely amazing.

> All authority in heaven and on earth has been given to me
> (Matt 28:18).

Jesus did not say that he had *some* authority. He said that *all* authority had been given to him. However, although he gained all authority on earth, he did not keep it.

Jesus gave authority on earth back to humans, who had lost it. That is amazing, but consistent with what God had done at the beginning. Humans responded in two different ways. Those who received the gospel responded to his gift of authority by accepting him as their Lord and surrendering authority over their lives back to him. Most people rejected the gospel and the gift of the Holy Spirit. They fell back under the powers of evil and lost the authority that Jesus had won back for them.

Jesus' death, resurrection and ascension brought a dramatic change in the authority situation on earth.

- Jesus ascended to a place of authority over the spiritual realms. This will never change, now or in the age to come.
- The spiritual powers of evil were defeated by the cross. They were cast out of heaven and made trespassers on earth. They can only retain authority by fooling people into rejecting the gospel and giving authority back to them.
- Followers of Jesus have authority over the powers of evil provided they remain united with Jesus. This gives them authority to heal the sick and cast out evil spirits that are oppressing people against their will.
- The people of the world are still under the authority of the powers of evil, because they lost the authority that Jesus returned to them when they rejected the gospel.
- Christians do not have authority over other humans, whether they are Christian or not. God does not give us authority over people. We only have authority over other people, if they freely submit to us.

The mixed response to this big authority shift explains the continuing spiritual struggle on earth. The Kingdom of God waxes and wanes according to the numbers on each side. During seasons when the gospel is effective, God has greater authority to act, and the powers of evil are squeezed out. But when the number of Christians declines, the powers of evil get a free reign.

The Times of the Gentiles

Jesus' ministry on earth started another season of struggle on earth. He called it the Times of the Gentiles (Luke 21:24), because most Jewish people would reject his new covenant and opt to remain under the Mosaic covenant. This covenant has magnificent promises, but since the temple was destroyed, no sacrifice for sin exists, so the Jewish people are stuck on the wrong side of a good covenant; caught under its curse and shut out of its blessings.

The spiritual forces of evil are expert accusers, so they demand the right to enforce the old covenant against the Jewish people. Although Jesus defeated the powers of evil on the cross, they still have authority to attack those under the old covenant.

The powers of evil have been able to do great evil on earth by attacking the people of the old covenant. During the Times of the Gentiles, they have used this last vestige of authority on earth, despite their defeat on the cross. This has held back the Kingdom of God for more than 2000 years.

Big Government

The Times of the Gentiles have been dominated by a variety of human governments. Now towards the end of this season, political power has been centralised and consolidated as never before. Expectations of political leaders are greater than ever, and they have demanded the power to deliver.

Concentration of political power leverages the authority of the powers of evil. By attacking the people at the top of the political hierarchy, the spiritual powers of evil gain authority over all the people submitted to them. They have gained immense authority on earth, despite their defeat on the cross, because people submit to leaders they control.

During the Times of the Gentiles, the following authority situation applies.

- Jesus released authority to those who trust in him. They have authority over their own lives and the areas of life under their authority.

- The devil and his angels have authority in the lives of the people deceived into rejecting Jesus' victory on the cross.
- The powers of evil have authority to attack the people living under the old covenant.
- Human political powers continue to exercise authority over the nations of the earth. The principalities and powers have authority over those who submit to political power.
- Christians do not have authority over kings and political powers. They are humans, so God wants them to be free.
- If kings and politicians have surrendered authority to evil spiritual powers, Christians do not have authority over the strongholds that they have established.

The fullness of the Government of God cannot come during the Times of the Gentiles, because the powers of evil are too strong.

The population of the world is greater than it has ever been, more than 7 billion people. The number of evil spirits at work in the world has not increased, since their rebellion at the beginning and a large number were locked up at the time of the flood. Because their number is fixed, they should now be weaker than they have ever been, as they have to spread themselves more thinly across the world.

However, they have amplified their limited authority by aligning themselves with political power. Because political power is more controlling and more widespread than it has ever been, this strategy has more than compensated them for their limited numbers. Consequently, they are probably more powerful than they have ever been. By supporting political power, we have strengthened the powers of evil, when they should be weak.

Towards the end of the Times of the Gentiles, political power will be expanded and centralised. This concentration of power will further empower the principalities and powers. A political empire described in the book of Revelation will be given immense authority by other political powers during a time of darkness on earth. The principalities and powers that control this empire will gain authority over much of the earth, as the people on earth submit to its authority.

Coming of the Kingdom

The last two obstacles to the Kingdom of God will be destroyed and overthrown during a Time of Distress that marks the end of the Times of the Gentiles.

- **Fullness of the Jews** - the Spirit of the Lord will be poured out, causing the Jewish people to cry out to Jesus for deliverance. The Holy Spirit will give them faith to receive the salvation that comes through grace.
- **Collapse of Big Government** - the events that release the Fullness of the Jews will lead to the destruction of human government and political empires throughout the world. Political powers will collapse and crumble. Politicians will flee their posts and sneak away. The destruction of human government will be so horrifying that the people of the world will never trust human political power again. Faith in political power will vanish forever.

These events produce a massive Authority Shift on earth.

- When the Jews move under the new covenant, the curses of the old covenant will lose their power. Jesus' sacrifice on the cross will cover their sins and provide full spiritual protection for them. The spiritual powers enforcing the curses of the old covenant will lose their power and have to go back to less effective methods.
- When big government is destroyed, political authority will shrivel, shrink and disappear. The principalities and powers that have amplified their power by controlling political authorities will lose their place. They will be reduced to ordinary evil spirits attacking one person at a time. As more and more people receive the gospel, this will become a very unrewarding task.

As the spiritual forces of evil disperse to deal with the authority that is diffused through society, they become fragmented and weak. Christians preaching the gospel in the power of the spirit will bind the spiritual powers and nullify their power.

This shift in authority will allow the Holy Spirit to bring the Kingdom of God to its promised fulfilment. The powers of evil will have lost their last scraps of authority on earth. Their rapid decline will open the way for the advance of the Kingdom of God (Rom 11:12).

The Holy Spirit will work in the hearts of all people to draw them to Jesus. As he teaches people to love and obey Jesus, all authority on earth will be brought into submission to him. The Government of God will come as the Holy Spirit guides people into Jesus' will on earth without force and coercion (Zech 4:6). The collapse of human government and the fullness of the Jews will radically change the authority situation on earth to remove the last obstacles to the kingdom of God.

As authority is returned to families and communities, political power will be chopped up, pushed down and spread around to ordinary people who trust Jesus and walk in the Spirit. The Holy Spirit will establish the Government of God using Free Authority. The governments of the world will disappear and be replaced by the Government of God.

18

Distress and Victory

Wait for God

The political institutions that dominate the modern world are obstacles to the fullness of the Kingdom of God, so they must be swept away before it comes. However, their authority is so entrenched in our culture that it seems like they will be around forever. We should not be intimidated by their power, but wait upon God. He will remove the power of human governments when his people are renewed by the gospel and the Spirit and ready to replace them with the Government of God.

In Jesus' time, the Roman Empire appeared to be invincible, but the gospel worked away out of sight. The empire eventually fell apart, but the church survived, grew stronger, and spread throughout the world. Unfortunately, when the empire collapsed in the fourth century, the church seized control and attempted to prop up the existing system. Christians were not ready with an alternative system of justice and defence, so a great opportunity for releasing the Kingdom of God was lost.

God's people must be prepared for the time when God allows human governments to collapse. Until that happens, we should ignore political power and get on with proclaiming the gospel and establishing neighbourhood churches. Trying to re-capture existing political institutions is a waste of time, because Imposed Authority cannot be made good.

Followers of Jesus should develop Kingdom Communities that can provide genuine welfare, justice and protection. They will be ready to fill the gap when governments fail.

Prophesy against Power

God does not want his people to fight the political powers, but in every age, he calls prophets to speak to nations and governments and challenge them. Prophets like Jeremiah and Miciah challenged the kings of Judah and Israel. Daniel confronted the emperors of Babylon and Persia. John warned of the collapse of the Roman Empire and all subsequent empires.

God is still calling prophets to warn human political powers that they will be swept away by events they cannot control. The end of the Times of the Gentiles will be marked by a short season of distress. Powerful governments will respond by demanding unprecedented powers to turn back the troubles. Some church leaders and prophets will support this accumulation of power, but they will lose their spiritual influence.

The true prophets will challenge the massive expansion of human government. They will warn of the dangers of Imposed Authority and pronounce God's judgement against the evil actions of the political powers. His prophets will also announce the destructive events that their conduct will inflict on their nations.

Many believers will suffer for their faith when politicians and leaders attack the prophets to stifle their voice. True prophets will stand firm in the face of this persecution and not be intimidated into silence. If they speak clearly, God will lift up their words and the people will hear, even if their rulers have stopped their ears.

Power Fail

Modern government is based on the idea that political power can constrain the effects of sin and evil, but this project has been a huge failure. Governments have gained immense power, but despite their best efforts, the world is still a mess.

- Modern political leaders are supported by thousands of bureaucrats, but without the wisdom of the Holy Spirit, they repeat stupid mistakes.
- People with political power continue to be corrupted. As the size of government has increased, the potential for corruption magnifies.
- The concentration of authority in a few people actually increases the scope for evil. The great evils of the twentieth century were the work of political powers.
- The modern state has not restored freedom, but needs more and more power and control.
- The modern state is synonymous with war. Wars have become horrendously harmful to innocent civilians.
- State power tends to destroy the cohesiveness of local communities.

Human government has had a good run, but it will eventually fail.

Empires Collapse

Christians do not need to fight against human political powers, because God will bring them down when the time is right.

> The court will sit for judgment, and his dominion will be taken away, annihilated and destroyed forever (Dan 7:26).

We should not try to destroy human political power, but wait for it to collapse under its own weight. God will sweep kingdoms and empires from the face of the earth.

> The God of heaven will set up a kingdom that will never be destroyed, nor will it be left to another people. It will crush all those kingdoms and bring them to an end, but it will itself endure forever (Dan 2:44).

The prophets looked forward to the time when empires and kings will be removed from the earth.

> The LORD Almighty has a day in store for all the proud and lofty, for all that is exalted (and they will be humbled). The arrogance of man will be brought low and human pride humbled; the LORD alone will be exalted (Isaiah 2:12,17).

During the time of distress, a great rush of political pride will climax in attempts to build a perfect government and spread its influence throughout the world. Hopes will be high, but trust in political power always leads to disaster. The arrogance of the political powers will collapse under the weight of failed promises.

The book of Revelation describes the destruction of the last human empire.

> The kingdom of the world has become
> the kingdom of our Lord and of his Messiah
> and he will reign for ever and ever (Rev 11:15).

During a season of economic and social crisis, the kingdoms of the world will be swept away and replaced by God's Kingdom.

Prepared for Distress

Until the season that God destroys political power, followers of Jesus will often be repressed by political rulers and governments. Emperors and governors have real political power, so fighting against them is pointless. Instead of revolting against unjust power, we will often need to submit to political power, so we can get on with proclaiming the good news.

When human governments start demanding excessive authority and power to deal with escalating calamity, followers should get together to protect themselves. They will be more secure, if they live close to others who are committed to supporting each other.

People standing alone can be picked off one by one. When the enemy is strong and God has been squeezed out of a city or nation, life will be dangerous for isolated Christians. They should come together for spiritual and physical protection. Groups of believers who understand authority should submit to each other and establish enclaves of safety in a dangerous world.

Neighbourhood churches led by elders with balanced giftings will survive and thrive during the season of distress. They will equip Christians to remain strong when the rest of society is collapsing.

A neighbourhood church will be fairly persecution proof. Because it does not depend on big leaders in large buildings, most political authorities would not realise it is a church. They will not be able to stop neighbours talking to each other and sharing meals together. A neighbourhood church will be visible to their neighbours, but invisible to the authorities.

When human governments collapse, an enormous vacuum will remain. Warlords and gangsters who have been undermining the government will look for opportunities to fill the gap. People looking for security and justice will not know where to turn. Neighbourhood churches will offer economic support and physical protection to everyone residing in their neighbourhood.

Equipped for Victory

If God's prophets have warned of the collapse of human political power, his people should be ready with a better way of organising society. Then when failed human systems are swept away, they can be replaced with God's government, not another human concoction.

Followers of Jesus should develop Kingdom Communities capable of providing the services that human governments promise, but fail to deliver. By developing out of sight, these communities will be functioning and ready to multiply when human governments collapse. They will serve their communities by providing social and economic support and protection from crime and violence.

God cannot remove the human political powers until his people are prepared to survive the distress and heal the broken world. A crisis can open people's hearts, but if no one is there to pour oil on their wounds, scars will harden them to the gospel. When the political powers fail, the remnant must be ready with an alternative culture to fill the gap.

God's new model for society must be up and operating when it is needed. People who are confused about the future will need to see it, before they will be willing to commit to it. A demonstration of the Government of God must be ready for when the world needs it. Kingdom Communities will provide an alternative model that desperate people can follow.

God's people should establish neighbourhood churches in strategic enclaves and gradually transform them into Kingdom Communities. The initial impact will be quite small, but these communities will be an example that other followers of Jesus can copy when the opportunity arises.

Rapid Growth

The Time of Distress will be a double whammy for the spiritual powers of evil. The collapse of human government will eliminate the ability of principalities and powers to control cities and nations. The Calling of the Jews will destroy their authority to attack the Jewish people still living under the old covenant. Without these two sources of authority, the powers of evil will be massively weakened.

The Holy Spirit will be free to move in power throughout the world and bring in a great harvest. Neighbourhood churches that have kept people safe from trouble and violence during a season of trouble and distress will be equally effective when the gospel is spreading quickly. They can absorb a large number of new Christians, as the gospel moves in the power of the Spirit.

A multitude of new believers will need discipling. God will not want any to fall away, because no one is ready to watch over them. If one of the elders is an evangelist, the rest of the team will share the gospel powerfully. If a couple of the elders are pastoral, they will ensure that people choosing to follow Jesus are discipled quickly and are soon ready for leadership. Apostolic elders will be constantly releasing new leaders in their place and moving out to establish new neighbourhood churches.

Neighbourhood churches led by teams of elders with balanced gifts will be essential for the rapid advance of the Kingdom. As the gospel is preached in the power of the Spirit, they will ensure that the new disciples are established in the body of Jesus and discipled to grow quickly. Massive growth will be absorbed by rapid multiplication of neighbourhood churches.

Kingdom Emerges

Authority will be chopped up, pushed down and spread around to families and communities. The new neighbourhood churches will transition into Kingdom Communities by offering everything that human governments have promised, but failed to deliver:

- food for the hungry
- relief from poverty
- spiritual protection

- protection from crime
- justice for the oppressed
- defence against attack.

Kingdom Communities will be held together by love and compassion, worked out in sharing and service. Participation will be voluntary. Elders will exercise Free Authority. People will be free to withdraw their submission at any time. If they think the leadership has turned sour, they will be free to ignore it, or leave the community.

Glorious Kingdom

The followers of Jesus will proclaim the gospel in the power of the Spirit and the people of the world will receive their message with gladness. As Kingdom Communities spread from neighbourhood to neighbourhood, region to region and nation to nation, the Kingdom of God will grow to fullness. All opposition to the gospel will be gone.

> The kingdom of the world has become the kingdom of our Lord and of his Messiah, and he will reign for ever and ever (Rev 11:15).

The kingdoms of the world will disappear and be replaced by the Government of God. It will be a glorious kingdom.

- The church will refined by suffering and become the beautiful and holy bride that John described (Rev 19:8).
- The spiritual forces of evil will remain on earth, skulking around powerless, seeking authority but not finding it.
- The Holy Spirit will be free to move without their opposition.
- The majority of people on the earth will receive the gospel and come to faith in Jesus (Psalm 22:27).
- The influence of sin will be massively reduced by the power of the Holy Spirit.
- When people see the glory of the Kingdom, God will be worshipped throughout the whole of the world.
- Human governments will be replaced by the local judges applying the law of God (Micah 4:1-5).

- Trust in Imposed Authority will be gone, so freedom will reign throughout the earth.
- Nationalism will be replaced by unity in Jesus.
- Wars will cease and be replaced by peace (Micah 4:3).
- Poverty will disappear as the earth yields a tremendous harvest (Micah 4:4).
- Selfishness and materialism will be replaced by simplicity and sharing. The poor will have more and the wealthy west will be content with less (Is 65:21-23).
- Sickness will retreat as the gospel advances. People will live out their full life span until their purpose on earth has been fulfilled.
- Creation will come into a glorious freedom of God. The earth will be restored when the powers of evil are prevented from devastating the physical world (Rom 8:19-21).

No Need to Wait

We do not know when the Time of Distress will come, and how long it will take, so we should be prepared at all times. The entire process might take as long as a couple of centuries. It certainly won't be done in seven years. Progress will not be smooth. There will be many setbacks on the way, but God will use the suffering of each defeat to birth another victory.

The transition will be quicker in some regions than others. As human government retreats towards the centres of power, people living on the margins of society or the edge of the city will be able to do something special. God's people should be prepared to take advantage of opportunities where and when they arise.

We do not need to wait for the collapse of big government to start building Kingdom Communities. A neighbourhood church can begin building alternative governing structures at any time. Rather than worrying about the coming distress, we should focus on serving Jesus and being prepared for the victory of his kingdom. Strong neighbourhood churches can be equipped for victory and prepared for distress.

About the Author

Ron McKenzie is a Christian writer
living in Christchurch, New Zealand.
During the 1980s, he served as
the pastor of a church,
but found that he did not fit that role.
He was employed as an economist
but has recently retired from that role.
He is married with three adult children
and several grandchildren.

By the Same Author

Being Church Where We Live

This challenging book offers a radical vision for the church that will stir hearts and provide guidance for people living through the Time of Distress and preparing for the glory of the Kingdom. It explains how society can be transformed from the bottom up.

Prophetic Ministry

The church urgently needs the release of the prophetic ministry. This book describes the operation of this important ministry in the church and nation.

Healing: Insights for Christian Elders

Healing the sick was crucial for the success of the early church. The modern Christian practice falls far short of their experience. This book provides fifteen keys that will help God's people obtain greater victory over pain and sickness.

Times and Seasons

This book takes a different approach to God's plan for history. It begins with the ministry of Jesus and the sending of the Holy Spirit and ends with the glory of the Kingdom of God. The key seasons and the epochal events that mark the change from each season to the next are clearly described.

Kingdom Authority

Jesus prayed that God's authority would be done on earth and it is in heaven. This raises a big question. How did the God who created the universe end up losing authority over the earth? What happened on earth and in heaven that meant his authority on earth has to be restored? How did Jesus restore his authority? To understand these questions, we must understand the working of authority and the big shifts in authority that have shaped history on earth. This book is a prequel to Government of God.

God's Economy

The emergence of the Government of God will bring radical change to society that feeds through into radical changes in the economy. These changes will be described in a sequel to the Government of God. The application of Kingdom principles will transform economic life in an amazing way.

www.ingramcontent.com/pod-product-compliance
Lightning Source LLC
Chambersburg PA
CBHW060749050426
42449CB00008B/1334